GERALD MORTIMER
ARE THE FIXTURES OUT?

GERALD MORTIMER
ARE THE FIXTURES OUT?

Evening
Telegraph

breedon **books**
PUBLISHING

First published in Great Britain in 2003 by
The Breedon Books Publishing Company Limited
Breedon House, 3 The Parker Centre,
Derby, DE21 4SZ.

ISBN 1 85983 378 0

Printed and bound by Butler & Tanner,
Frome, Somerset, England.

Cover printing by Lawrence-Allen Colour Printers,
Weston-super-Mare, Somerset, England.

CONTENTS

FOREWORD
by Roy McFarland

I know how important sport is to the people of Derbyshire, how strongly they feel about Derby County Football Club and Derbyshire Cricket Club.

Though I was born in Liverpool, I count Derby as my home having spent the majority of the last 36 years living here.

I have seen at first hand the lift that both clubs can give the City and the County.

Gerald Mortimer's words and considered thoughts through the pages of the *Derby Evening Telegraph* have played a big part in that.

He fed the public news and views from the football and cricket clubs for more than 30 years, reporting on the good and not so good times of both, particularly Derby County.

He was there throughout the successes of the Seventies when the Baseball Ground buzzed with anticipation, especially on those great European nights.

He was there throughout the dark days of the early Eighties when the club stared bankruptcy and the very real threat of extinction in the face, and he was there when the club bounced back in the late Eighties, before spending six years in the Premiership from the mid-Nineties until relegation at the end of 2001-02.

Gerald was there during all those key moments in the club's rich history.

I have known him for more than 30 years and consider him a friend. His passion for football and cricket has always burned brightly. He has great knowledge of Derby County and Derbyshire cricket, and a feel for the history of both clubs that certainly comes across in his writing.

I hope this book is a success for Gerald and that football and cricket followers throughout Derbyshire enjoy reading it.

I am sure they will!

INTRODUCTION

THE title popped up before I wrote a word because, for 32 years, my working life was ruled by two sets of fixtures. When the football schedule appeared in June, the first glance was always towards Christmas and New Year to see what unpleasant journeys the planners would offer. During the summer, the greater interest was in venues, although four-day cricket, sadly, reduced the number of 'out' grounds.

The job at the *Derby Evening Telegraph* was seldom dull. During my time, Derby County were twice League Champions, were relegated four times and promoted three times. They are at their most vulnerable when enjoying success, as proved by the way Brian Clough and Dave Mackay lasted only 18 months each after lifting the Championship trophy. Even now, those decisions defy rational explanation but Derbyshire cricket was equally wayward.

The team that won the first NatWest Trophy, on the most emotionally draining day I ever spent in a Press box, started to break up before they left Lord's. After a long rebuilding process, Derbyshire followed victory in the Refuge Assurance League with a memorable triumph in the Benson and Hedges Cup. Again, the team disintegrated, good players going off to help other counties. There must be something in the Derby water and the only lesson to emerge from these pages is that the city's two major clubs never learn. Both were in a parlous condition as I struggled to adjust to retirement.

Reflection on events since 1970 involved much revisiting and moments of alarm as instant judgements were proved to be fallacious. That is the lot of every commentator, whether the medium is written or verbal, but there was a unique chance to gain knowledge in my early years at the *Telegraph* by listening to Brian Clough and Peter Taylor. They were better than any lecturers at Oxford University, largely because they made their subject so easy to grasp. Exactly the same principles brought them even greater success with Nottingham Forest, hard though that was for Derby people to stomach.

Over the years, many managers, players and supporters of both games became friends. My small part in floating the Derby County Former Players' Association helped to preserve those friendships and bring lasting pleasure. I have, too, valued the camaraderie of journalists. All are potential rivals and often pass like ships in the night but there is a shared experience, a world to which Press box free-loaders do not have entry. Many people helped me and several are mentioned in these pages. I hope some of that assistance was returned, although the box at the County Ground had the reputation of being a trap for the unwary: good professionals had no worries.

Putting this together revived many memories, of bad days as well as good ones, and I hope they will mean something to those kind enough to buy this book.

Gerald Mortimer
September 2003

FROM A WINDOW
ON THE SPOT

ONLY one cast was needed to hook this fish. On January 12, 1946, I was taken to the Baseball Ground for the first time to see Derby County play Millwall. Angus Morrison scored three times, Raich Carter twice in an 8-1 victory and, although I was hardly aware of it at the time, this was a first glimpse of one of Derby County's most distinguished teams. It is impossible to recall how much a nine-year-old absorbed but there was a desire to return, something that never left me, even after the move to Pride Park. This was the season of the FA Cup victory but it took years to acquire the knack of searching out Wembley tickets. My family was not into football and did not have the contacts, then as now the key. I suppose I listened to a commentary on the wireless, a strange name given the number of wires needed to extract life from our set, and in all probability Raymond Glendenning was pouring out words. He was a portly man with a handlebar moustache and a celebrity in his day. Accuracy mattered little because, apart from a few glimpses on cinema newsreels, there was no way of checking. Happily, film survives of the Wembley victory over Charlton Athletic and, in recent times, watchers at Former Players' Association dinners have gasped at the way wing-halves Jim Bullions and Chick Musson left their imprint on the opening minutes, letting Charlton know this was to be a proper game. It was an eventful occasion because the game went into extra-time, Bert Turner is credited with scoring for both sides and the ball burst as Jack Stamps was about to test Charlton goalkeeper Sam Bartram.

There was closer contact for those who did not make it to Wembley when Jack Nicholas and the team brought the Cup back to Derby. A brewers' dray was decorated for the occasion and, through a friend of a friend, I had a vantage point at the upper window of a shop on The Spot as the heroes moved slowly towards Full Street police station. A few days later, several of the players attended a swimming gala at Queen Street baths and patiently signed autographs. It was a curiously low key occasion and it is impossible to imagine modern Cup winners going to such an event without being overwhelmed by the crowd, not to mention being handsomely paid for their trouble. At the end of the season, Derby met Charlton again in the League South, an extension of the wartime competition that bridged the gap until the Football League began again in 1946-47. The gates were closed with me on the outside, so I went home and chucked the programme on the garden bonfire. Silly me but who could then have predicted the boom in football memorabilia?

On a few occasions that season, the Rams had a goalkeeper called Savage (Queen of the South). In my ignorance, I knew nothing of the club in Dumfries and in equal innocence assumed the tag in brackets to be a nickname. Even without later connotations attached to 'queen', Reg Savage would have been unimpressed had he known those thoughts. He was one of the guest players all teams used during World War Two. Those who entered the aborted 1939-40 season were liable to be scattered far from home on armed service, there were obvious restrictions on travelling and players slipped in for a game where and when they could. Derby did well out of the system because it brought them the two greatest inside forwards of the 1930s. Raich Carter, who had married a Derby girl, and Peter Doherty were stationed at an RAF rehabilitation centre in Loughborough. They agreed to guest for the Rams and those able to attend the Baseball Ground had their horizons extended. Carter and Doherty were so good that it was like a regular course in the arts of football. Years later, I asked Tim Ward, an England international as a Derby player and later manager, if my unformed schoolboy impressions of the two had any relevance.

Carter, with his distinctive silver hair, always seemed a magisterial player, directing games from a space he apparently carried around and thumping in shots that offered goalkeepers little hope of making a save. He did not always bother to see the outcome because he knew he had scored. Doherty, red-haired and equally easy to pick out, was more inclined to run, with or without the ball. He was always on the move, dribbling past opponents, passing, looking for the return, shooting. Ward, to my pleasure, accepted the general assessment in his courteous way. He loved them as players but was especially close to Raich. Arthur Cox, who managed the Rams to promotions in successive seasons, worked with Doherty at Preston North End and Sunderland. At those clubs, Cox would listen to Peter's stories of how he put so much into every match that he was often still in the bath when the groundsman wanted to lock up and go home.

Carter guested for Derby as a Sunderland player and Doherty was with Manchester City. They had won the Championship with their clubs and Carter led Sunderland to their first FA Cup success. They could play for Derby in the League South but, in 1945-46 with hostilities at an end, only registered players could appear in the FA Cup. Derby cut it fine but, in December, 1945, Carter and Doherty were signed. The total outlay was something like £12,000 and, through those deals, Derby put one hand on the Cup. Ted Magner, manager until he handed over to Stuart McMillan, deserves much credit, as does the chairman, Ben Robshaw. In the early part of the Second World War, Derby were found guilty of making illegal payments during the 1930s, thus explaining how they were able to keep so many talented players. Robshaw, other directors and George Jobey, the manager, were suspended *sine die*, although few believed that other clubs were not equally guilty in the days of a maximum wage. Happily for Robshaw, the suspension was lifted and he returned as chairman. Brian Clough used to say Robshaw was the best to hold that office at Derby – 'because he looked after the players'. Another suspension followed, over payments on a post-season tour, but Robshaw fulfilled his dream at Wembley. Chairmen, like managers, are measured by success.

It was inevitable that Derby's Cup team did not stay together long. Seven of the Wembley winners played before war broke out in 1939 and

Jack Nicholas made his debut in 1928, at which time Dally Duncan was setting out with Hull City. When Duncan died in Brighton in 1990, at the age of 80, I wrote an obituary for the *Derby Evening Telegraph* and later received a very pleasant note from his son, who observed that he had not appreciated how much the Wembley victory still meant in Derby. That continues to hold good, although many who saw it have passed on. Age was against that team but Derby could have kept Doherty for longer. He wanted to take over the Arboretum Hotel and was bitterly disappointed by the reaction of the directors, who thought it might have an adverse effect on his play. Doherty knew they misread his character and moved to Huddersfield Town before going into management with Doncaster Rovers, Bristol City and, his most spectacular success, Northern Ireland. Carter became player-manager of Hull City and had the fans cramming into the recently constructed Boothferry Park. To replace them, Derby twice paid British record fees, £15,500 to Greenock Morton for Billy Steel and £24,500 to Manchester United for Johnny Morris. Steel, who played in Great Britain's 6-1 victory over Rest of Europe at Hampden Park in May, 1947, had abundant talent but was also a disruptive influence. His contemporaries said little at the time, although several important players moved on, but were more forthcoming in later life.

They reckoned Steel gave his best in London, knowing that influential journalists would be there, or when there was a Scotland game in the offing. Claims that a Scottish selector was at the ground often surfaced in an attempt to provoke Steel into displaying his skill. At least the Rams showed a profit when he moved to Dundee for £23,000 after three years at Derby. Morris, an FA Cup winner in Matt Busby's first great Manchester United team, started brilliantly after Derby signed him, scoring 13 goals in his 13 games at the end of 1948-49 and winning an England place. He was clever on the ball, powerful in front of goal and a tough competitor. I saw some of those early games but should explain that, until the late 1960s, my visits to the Baseball Ground were, of necessity, intermittent. I was a boarder at Repton, both the Prep School and the senior school, until 1955 before doing two years of National Service in the Sherwood Foresters. During the second year in the army, I watched a good deal of football in

Germany and formed a particular attachment to Borussia Dortmund, then the Champions. They played in the Liga West because regional competitions still prevailed, culminating in a Meisterschaft for the various champions. In this way, I was able to see most of the players who won the World Cup for Germany in 1954. Helmut Rahn, a muscular winger who scored twice in the victory over Hungary, provided a particular memory at Dortmund's Rote-Erde Stadion. Rahn, playing for Rot-Weiss Essen, was famous for his powerful shooting and let fly from outside the penalty area. Hans Kwiatkowski, in the Borussia goal, had time only to react with his fists. It was a jab rather than a punch but the ball soared away to bounce in the centre circle.

After completing my stint with the Foresters, I was at Oxford for three years and taught English for 10 years. Not until 1968 was I clear of boarding side duties and, happily, that freedom coincided with the Brian Clough and Peter Taylor Second Division Championship side. For much of the intervening period, Derby County were either in decline or meandering in Division Two, unambitious and failing to engender much in the way of excitement. I played a fair amount, not particularly well, and savoured some of the outposts of the Midland Amateur Alliance with one of the Derbyshire Amateurs' teams, then so splendidly organised by Jack Whitaker while he was running the Royal School for the Deaf in Friar Gate.

In the immediate post-war years, Derby reached a Cup semi-final in 1948, losing to Manchester United at Hillsborough, and were third in Division One the following year. From that point, they began to slide as the quality of the playing staff declined. Although Stuart McMillan managed Derby to Wembley success with what was essentially Ted Magner's team, he seemed passive from the outside. He had a good pedigree because his father John played 126 games for the Rams in Steve Bloomer's time before moving to Leicester Fosse, Small Heath (now Birmingham City), Bradford City and Glossop. John managed Gillingham after World War One and, after one appearance for the Rams, Stuart played for him there in a career that took in Chelsea, without any senior games, Wolverhampton Wanderers, Bradford City, Nottingham Forest and Clapton Orient. He had been out of football for some time, although doing some scouting and ferrying directors to games, when the Rams asked him, in January, 1946, to stop pulling pints at the Nag's Head, Mickleover, and manage the club. McMillan fell on his feet because, in a season of reorganisation in the football world, he had only to toss the ball to Nicholas and watch Carter and Doherty running out to know Derby had a good chance, whoever the opposition.

They were long gone when, in 1952-53, the Rams lost the First Division place they had maintained since promotion under George Jobey in 1925-26. As they floundered in the Second Division, Derby called time on McMillan in November, 1953, and he returned to the licensed trade, this time at the Station Hotel, Ashbourne. He was a fine games player, cricket for Derbyshire, a county golfer and a high-class billiards player, but probably not a forceful manager. In his place, Derby engaged Jack Barker, one of their greatest players from the 1930s. Barker was a centre-half who, despite the change in the offside law and consequent development of the stopper, had an eye to attack. He was renowned for sweeping long and accurate passes out to Sammy Crooks and Dally Duncan on the wings. Barker won 11 caps for England and was captain on his last appearance but neither enjoyed nor made a success of his time as a manager. He averted the threat of relegation in 1954 but, a year later, Derby dropped out of the Second Division for the first time in their history. I remember a match at the Baseball Ground in April, 1955, as possibly the most depressing of my life. Swansea Town won 4-1 on a dry, dusty surface in the third of what turned out to be seven consecutive defeats for Derby. Division Three North beckoned and, clearly, the towel had gone in. That the team contained some who gave the Rams tremendous service – Geoff Barrowcliffe, Frank Upton, Tommy Powell, Jack Parry, Ray Young – serves only to emphasise the importance of organisation, morale, leadership, having a club as opposed to a few players. I have been thoroughly cast down by Derby County on a number of occasions since then but never to quite the same extent. But Derby do this. Nine years after winning the FA Cup, they were on their way to the Third North: nine years after their second League Championship, they prepared to spend their Centenary Year in Division Three. 'Derby' and 'stability' do not sit well in the same sentence.

The other place to be discovered in the 1940s was the County Ground but I have no clear recollection of my first sight of county cricket. In 1946, the first summer after World War Two, Derbyshire were led by Gilbert Hodgkinson and relied heavily on the players whose careers were interrupted in 1939. Hodgkinson, who owned a flower shop at the bottom of Green Lane in Derby, was essentially a useful club cricketer and remarkable only in that he was able to read his own obituary, published in a wartime *Wisden* after he was posted as 'missing, believed dead' while serving with the Sherwood Foresters. Hodgkinson found the captaincy a strain and, for 1947, was succeeded by Eddie Gothard, a Burton club player who was 42 when he first stepped on a county field. There were some experienced professionals remaining from Derbyshire's 1936 Championship team and, a decade further on, not all were easy to handle. Stan Worthington, who went to Australia in Gubby Allen's 1936-37 team, was commissioned during the war and, as Hodgkinson's vice-captain, felt he was worth more serious consideration for the leadership. In all probability, he was right but Derbyshire continued to be led by amateurs until Charlie Lee was appointed in 1963. One of Gothard's briefs was to impose greater discipline while bringing in some new players. Not that the pre-war players were washed up. Bill Copson, who took to cricket only to fill in time during the general strike of 1926, was a fine natural bowler in the Derbyshire tradition, not quite genuinely fast but fast enough, and certainly hostile enough, to be an awkward proposition. Like Worthington, he went to Australia in 1936-37 but consistent performances in the State games failed to secure him a Test place. He did, however, become one of those who played for England before and after the war when he was picked against South Africa in 1947, one of three Derbyshire players to take the new ball in that series. Another was George Pope, as good an all-rounder as any to represent the county. Pope was tall, bald and exuding competitive spirit. His talent was not always used on Derbyshire's behalf, because he fancied the rewards of League cricket and after completing the double, 1,000 runs and 100 wickets, in 21 matches in 1948, never again played for the county. Pope was then 37 but became a legend with Sheffield United CC over a period of many years.

The third picked by England in 1947 was Cliff Gladwin, a medium-paced inswing bowler of unfailing accuracy who was remarkably light on his feet for such a big man. Gladwin made his Derbyshire debut in 1939 but without success, so he was 30 when he took his first wicket in 1946. A year later, another name appeared on the scorecard for the first time, that of Les Jackson at the age of 26. The heroes for my generation were in place as they dominated the Derbyshire attack. Gladwin, who retired in 1958, took 1,536 wickets for the county at 17.67 each: Jackson went on until 1963 and passed his partner with 1,670 at 17.11. Early memories of Derbyshire feature aggressive bowling, hostile fields and dour batsmen who made enough runs to give the bowlers time to be about their business. The batting gained enterprise when, in 1950, Arnold Hamer was engaged from the Yorkshire Leagues. He always went for his strokes as an opener, bolstered by a fatalism that told him there was a greater power at work. If it was his day, he would succeed, if not he would fail so, in the meantime, he might as well set about entertaining spectators. Although Gothard was no great shakes as a cricketer, he led the team for two seasons and managed two memorable feats. In 1947, he performed the hat-trick against Middlesex, who went on to win the Championship in the golden summer of Denis Compton (3,816 runs, average 90.85) and Bill Edrich (3,539, 80.43). Edrich was one of Gothard's bag at the County Ground, along with Alan Fairbairn and Walter Robins, a former England captain: not bad for gentle medium. In 1948, Gothard bowled Don Bradman when one of the great Australian teams visited Derby. That match attracted vast crowds, estimated at around 10,000, and I sat in awe. There was no television then, no overseas players flitting in and out of the county game so, for the people of Derby, it was the first chance to see Bradman and the Aussies since 1938. Matches against touring teams continued to be major occasions into the 1960s and 1970s but, since then, appear to have turned into a chore for both sides. It is sad, like so many changes in cricket. One to be particularly regretted is the decline in out-grounds, away from headquarters. Derbyshire had two main venues, the County Ground and Queen's Park, Chesterfield. In addition, on a regular cycle, they visited Burton, Buxton and Ilkeston. Queen's Park is a setting to make people fall in love with cricket but, through stubbornness on both sides, Derbyshire no longer go there. They should, however well the County Ground has developed.

I gained a more personal involvement in Derbyshire's affairs during my early terms at Repton because Guy Willatt joined the staff. He was a Nottingham man who was educated at Repton, played for his native county, captained Cambridge University in 1947 and represented Scotland while teaching at the Edinburgh Academy, combining this with reeling off centuries, once including five in successive weekends, for the Grange Club, where Derbyshire played a NatWest Trophy tie in 1998. He always believed that his Scotland cap was stolen by a Nationalist, upset at this English involvement. Derbyshire wangled a remarkable deal with Repton as, after joining the staff for the 1950 winter term, Willatt would spend four years, from 1951 to 1954, as captain, meaning that a substitute had to be found for the summer terms. In the last month of the 1950 season, Willatt was due to take over from Pat Vaulkhard but, on his debut, had a finger broken in the second over of the innings, hit on the hand by Warwickshire bowler Charlie Grove. That was the end of his cricket for the summer so Vaulkhard, once dropped by Willatt on his way to 264 against Nottinghamshire at Trent Bridge, stayed in office with hardly a blip. A year later, in my summer holiday, I went to see Derbyshire play Essex at the Ind Coope ground in Burton, where a lively pitch was virtually guaranteed. Willatt was an early casualty, bowled off his body by Ken Preston. A few minutes later, an elderly couple occupied the seats next to me and asked if Willatt was out. In explaining how it happened, how unlucky he was and that he was one of my teachers, there was a distinct buzz of adolescent hero-worship. The couple turned out to be Willatt's parents so, fortunately, the right things were said: what a polite young man, they may have thought. Whether or not Repton felt they had a good deal was not revealed but Willatt, having led Derbyshire to third place in 1954, then left to become headmaster of Heversham Grammar School in Westmorland. I was later on his staff there after a preliminary interview that took place while we watched Nottingham Forest from the Trent End terraces. Derbyshire did not reach such a high position in the Championship again until 1991, by which time Willatt was chairman of cricket and Kim Barnett the captain.

GET FELL IN

THE instruction had been there for some time. On 29 September, 1955, I was to report to Normanton Barracks to start two years of National Service with the Sherwood Foresters so, as the gate was about to clang shut, a midweek match at the Baseball Ground was the only sensible option. Derby County, relegated in my final school year, were in the Third Division North for the first time in their history. Dropping a division always feels like the end of the world but two years in the Third North proved to be great fun, although army duties condemned me to following much of it from a distance. The Rams scored goals, 110 and 111 in successive seasons. As comparatively recent FA Cup winners, they were an attraction wherever they went and Baseball Ground attendances stood up well, an average of more than 19,000. It was an early lesson in the loyalty of Derby followers and as, in those days, a proportion of gate receipts went to the away team, other clubs were delighted to have them in the division. The decision, taken in 1983, to allow home clubs to keep all the gate money is a defining moment in Football League history. From being a corporate organisation, even if bigger clubs always carried greater influence, the League admitted greed through the door and the breakaway to the Football Association Premiership, cornering the wealth, was, in the long run, a logical conclusion.

On the evening before my date at Normanton Barracks, Derby beat York City 3-2, Alf Ackerman scoring twice and Jesse Pye once. Both had been signed by Jack Barker in an attempt to preserve Second Division status but neither played a major part when promotion was secured. Pye, who had a fine record with Wolverhampton Wanderers, was 34 when he joined Derby and his best days were behind him. Harry Storer, who took over as manager at Derby's lowest ebb, used to say of Ackerman: "He could only play at home." Storer wanted more. I went to the York game with a school friend, Roger Gillard, and his father Ernest, who taught at Derby School for many years. He resembled Chalky White, the schoolmaster in Giles' cartoons, but was a totally delightful man who was accorded great respect and affection by generations who passed through that excellent school. Roger was due to report with me the following day but was later discovered, while on the firing range, to have an ear complaint that made him unsuitable for infantry service. He was transferred to Catterick Camp, where he spent the remainder of his army time playing football and cricket at a high standard. The experience he gained from associating with young professionals helped him to a football blue when he went to Oxford University as a post-graduate. Eddie Colman, one of the Manchester United stars killed in the Munich air crash, and Jimmy Melia, who won an England cap while with Liverpool, were among Gillard's contemporaries on the Yorkshire moors, along with Alan Smith, a future England wicket-keeper, and Ken Scotland, a rugby union international with Scotland. Nobody was exempt so, for example, Matt Busby had to rely on a station commander's good will to have Duncan Edwards regularly available for Manchester United in that two-year period. A few complimentary tickets surely helped the cause.

The logical way to arrive at Normanton Barracks was to take a taxi from the home I felt I was leaving for ever. The corporal on guard duty assumed a young officer was arriving and saluted smartly but changed his tone abruptly when he was made aware of my status. Kit was handed out that day, including the uncomfortable 'drawers, jungle green', and a diffident complaint that one pair of pyjamas did not match provoked an incendiary reaction, starting fortissimo and rising in volume. "Match? Match? You'll be wanting them to f***** fit next." On the first Sunday, the Church Parade was preceded by a brisk order: "Roman Catholics and other denominations, fall out." The rest of us briefly wondered if we'd been right to fill in

Church of England on our forms but the implied promise of services for each denomination turned out to be a lie. The fallers-out were found jobs, fatigues in army language, around the barracks. The home of the Sherwood Foresters was only ever a staging post for me. The intake was soon split on educational grounds and those with a reasonable hand of O and A levels were graded as Potential Officers and send to the Midland Brigade at Budbroke Barracks, Warwick, to join similar bright young things from the Lincolnshire, Leicestershire and Warwickshire Regiments with the aim of preparing for the War Office Selection Board (WOSB). The journey from Derby to Warwick was agony because possessions had to be enclosed in a kit bag and an array of packs and pouches known as Full Service Marching Order. While this was reasonably effective, putting everything together was a work of art and, with a change of stations in Birmingham, between New Street and Snow Hill, few of us dared to take off the apparatus in order to sit comfortably. In the winter of 1955-56, the train trip from Derby to Warwick became familiar and I used to look enviously at warmly lit windows in, if truth were told, unattractive areas of Birmingham.

I sustained one very useful injury in my time at Warwick when I was kicked under the foot in a football match against a Royal Artillery unit. It was inflicted by Gunner Brian Parsons, who already had a Cambridge cricket blue and was later to play for Surrey. As the match was on a Friday, the sensible decision was to go home for the weekend and report sick on Monday. New Street to Snow Hill on the return trip was a painful hobble but the medical services easily spotted the trouble, so a broken metatarsal demanded plaster and an office job at what was not only the coldest part of the winter but one which featured several potentially unpleasant exercises out of barracks. Diligence in making sure the coke stove was glowing when the others reappeared, cold and wet, was met by scorn. "It would have been too tough for you," they said, heroes returning from the front. They may well have been right but, happily, it was not put to the test. With a leg in plaster, I attended a match that is the indisputable low point in Derby County's history.

They were doing well in the Third North and, after knocking out Crook

Town in a replay, the FA Cup second round draw brought them against Boston United of the Midland League. More than half the Boston team were former Derby players under their player-manager Ray Middleton, goalkeeper and Justice of the Peace, the man who insured his hands for £2,000 when he was working as a miner. Middleton's best day were with Chesterfield, where his consistency was rewarded with four England B caps. With him were Reg Harrison, an FA Cup winner with Derby in 1946, and others who made less impact at the Baseball Ground – Dave Miller, the Hazledine brothers, Don and Geoff, Ray Wilkins. Incredibly, Boston won 6-1, one of the most startling Cup victories by a non-League side, and Geoff Hazledine, who appeared only once for the Rams, whipped in three goals. Derby were offered a chance to even the score in 1974 when, having been slightly fortunate to hold Boston to a 0-0 draw at the Baseball Ground, they won 6-1 at York Street, the scene of Archie Gemmill's only hat-trick for the Rams. Middleton was still around, by then Boston's secretary.

WOSB was held at Andover, in Hampshire, and featured the usual tests, impromptu lectures and taking oil drums over an imaginary river with planks that did not bridge the gap. Passing meant a more comfortable life in prospect but first Eaton Hall, on the Duke of Westminster's estate near Chester, had to be negotiated. It had a bad reputation because a number of struggling officer cadets committed suicide over the years. That was hard to understand because, whatever the problems, National Service was only two years in a young life and being returned to unit (RTUd) was hardly the end of the world. Sure, it was a daunting 16 weeks but, a useful lesson for football managers, team spirit flourishes under a strict regime. My former housemaster at Repton, Bernard Thomas, summed it up when, in 1957, I was about to enter the teaching profession and sought advice. "They like to know where they stand," he said. So it was with the army. When the Regimental Sergeant Major at Eaton Hall, Desmond Lynch, appeared on the parade ground, a vision of creases, glittering brass, boots with a mirror surface and overwhelming presence, it was not only the cadets who quailed. The NCOs scuttled around, while trying not to be noticed by the great man. I first met Bryon Butler at Eaton Hall and saw him at Stamford Bridge after Lynch's obituaries were published, provoking similar memories for both of us. Butler was the BBC's football correspondent, with a great voice for broadcasting, and also a gifted writer on the game, although he always wished he could have devoted more time to covering cricket. Even after a gap of around 40 years, we remained in awe of Lynch and we probably undertook the same pilgrimage in Chester, a visit to the Dublin Packet Inn. It was a spit and sawdust pub but was run by Dixie Dean, the greatest of all Everton centre-forwards, and the autograph I sought remains with me.

After surviving Eaton Hall, I emerged as a National Service officer and returned briefly to Normanton Barracks where Tony Pickard, the post-corporal, was still playing tennis against the Commanding Officer. Pickard, from Ripley, was a Davis Cup player who earned even greater distinction as a coach, especially in his guidance of Stefan Edberg. He had his National Service programme sorted out and I also made an important discovery about the Royal Army Dental Corps. The officer who was examining teeth came in for lunch and sank a formidable succession of neat gins before eating. Moral: have a morning appointment. Then it was off to join the battalion in Sennelager, Westphalia, after another train journey, this time with a sea trip from Harwich to the Hook of Holland. We were given colours so, provided the green train was boarded, arrived in Paderborn station. We were on a large training ground, once used by the German army, and the opportunities for travel were considerable. Hamburg and Berlin were the favourite outings, for a specialised aspect of German life, but my main destination soon became Dortmund, in the Ruhr. Borussia were the best team in the regional Liga West and I can still rattle off their regular 11. And the games were good occasions, with the sausage stalls offering a level of pre-match food never equalled in this country. After the regional leagues were completed, there was a play-off, the Endrunde. Kaiserslautern, the team of the Walter brothers, played Hertha Berlin in Wuppertal and the best way to the Stadion am Zoo was by overhead railway that followed the course of the river. The only fatalities were in the war, they told me, when the train stopped during a bombing raid which involved the inevitable blackout and passengers, thinking they were at a station, stepped out to plunge into the river. Kaiserslautern won 14-1, which remains the highest score I have seen although Tottenham Hotspur, 13-2 winners over Crewe Alexandra in an FA Cup replay, and Derby County's 12-0 dismissal of Finn Harps in the UEFA Cup ran it close. My year in Germany coincided with Derby's promotion but leave and a course at the Small Arms School in Hythe meant I was not a total absentee. In the spring of 1957, I had two charts going, one by then on the down slope showing weeks served and weeks remaining: the other encompassed fixtures for Derby and their rivals, most notably Hartlepools United and Accrington Stanley. A Foresters major, Cliff Bokenham, was a long time enthusiast and from a distance we savoured a vital Easter Monday result: Derby County 7, Chesterfield 1, with a crowd of 29,886. As gin, for example, was only five old pence a tot (about 2p), we did the occasion and Ray Straw's hat-trick justice.

The key to Derby's return from the dead was the appointment of Harry Storer in July, 1955. Although he was born in Liverpool, where his father was keeping goal, Storer's Derbyshire roots were strong. His father, Harry senior, made a fleeting appearance for Derbyshire at cricket and his uncle William was a Derbyshire and England wicketkeeper-batsman. The future manager joined the Rams as a player in 1921, from Grimsby Town, and made 274 appearances, as well as winning two England caps, before moving to Burnley. In addition, Storer played in 302 matches for Derbyshire between 1920 and 1936 as an opening batsman. Will Taylor, the secretary from 1908 to 1959, reckoned Storer was the best of all Derbyshire batsmen and, uniquely, he was already manager of Coventry City when he was involved in the 1936 County Championship success. He was, too, an experienced manager, taking Coventry and Birmingham to promotions, but had been out of the game for 18 months before Derby appointed him. Not that he was in the shadows, because he was a pungent contributor to the radio discussion programme *Sport in the Midlands*. Aware of the need to rebuild the club, Storer immediately signed a captain, Paddy Ryan from West Bromwich Albion for £3,000 only 14 months after he was an FA Cup winner. Manager and captain worked well together, building a necessary spirit. Ryan was one of the early members of the

Former Players' Association and always arrived early for the dinners, asking if any of the North side, as he put it, would be there. Storer went for another known quantity in centre-half Martin McDonnell, a tough enthusiast he had previously signed for Birmingham and Coventry, but also made use of many players already on the books. He gave goalkeeper Terry Webster his best two years in football, saw the potential of Geoff Barrowcliffe, Albert Mays, Jack Parry, Tommy Powell and Ray Straw. Derby might have gone up in 1955-56 had Parry not been injured by Ray de Gruchy in the key game against Grimsby Town. At the time, Parry had 24 League goals in 34 games but his season was over and Grimsby took the one promotion spot. When Derby followed them 12 months later, Straw equalled Jack Bowers' club record with 37 League goals. Like Barrowcliffe, Straw was a product of Ilkeston Town and a miner in the days when collieries were major employers there. Both spent their lives in the town and Straw was a king in the air for the Rams. Storer made sure he had the right service. Powell, who first appeared as a 16-year-old during the war, was essentially an inside-forward but Storer played him wide to make maximum use of his immaculate control and delivery. Tommy, educated at Bemrose School, became one of Derby's most loved players and, like his son Steve, passed 400 appearances. Both were one-club men and, for many years, Tommy worked in the accounts department at the *Derby Evening Telegraph* while buying a season-ticket at the Baseball Ground because he hated to be dependent on anyone else. He would reminisce about his playing partners but only up to a point. Tommy kept his confidences until the day he died, on his way back from a supporters' function, because that was the way he behaved. There was a deeply emotional moment when his funeral cortege paused outside the Baseball Ground and was respectfully applauded by supporters. As with Reg Harrison, it was a bad idea to walk through Derby in his company if you were in a hurry: both had time for everybody and everybody wanted a word.

Storer added experience during the first Third North season, such as Roy Martin, a composed left-back from Birmingham, and Dennis Woodhead to play on the left wing. Woodhead, a flight engineer who was involved in around 30 bombing missions in World War Two, made his name with Sheffield Wednesday before a brief spell at Chesterfield. On his debut, he launched a ferocious volley that skimmed the bar and got the crowd on his side, in the way that Spencer Prior's first, crunching tackle did when Jim Smith signed him to replace Christian Dailly in the 1990s.

While I was in Germany, I had a young Derby County player, Brian Daykin, as my batman. Daykin was permanently excused boots, because of bunions, and taking him under my wing was a good way to keep him out of trouble: it is fair to say that Dayk was not a natural soldier but was amusing company. He enabled me to complete the before and after National Service circle by providing a complimentary ticket on the day after my release, for a 3-2 home win over Lincoln City. It was not a total farewell to Normanton Barracks, as there were a few cricket matches in later years and, with severe consequences, a sherry party. When the Rams took off under Brian Clough and Peter Taylor, the barracks was used for 'park-and-ride' purposes. There was some retrospective pleasure in leaving a car on the drill square after frequently sweating round that area but, following amalgamation with the Worcestershire Regiment, Normanton Barracks disappeared and is now the site of something called the Forresters' Centre, with its inexplicable mis-spelling. So much for history. Promotion in 1957 proved an end in itself because Storer was unable to take the Rams further, nor was his successor, Tim Ward. We were in for a spell of Second Division ordinariness, with the occasional highlight. Storer provided one by signing George Darwin from Mansfield Town in 1957. Darwin, a running inside or centre-forward, had a brilliant first season when he scuttled over the notorious Baseball Ground mud. While it clawed at the feet of other players and, by all accounts, smelt evil, Darwin hardly touched the surface and was an entertainment in his own right. Ward offered another by paying Swansea Town £6,000 for Eddie Thomas, who equalled a Rams record by scoring in his first six League games and formed a prolific partnership with Alan Durban. When, in 1967, Ward found his contract would not be renewed, he half-regretted his shrewdness in signing Thomas because directors then expected 20 goals in a season for peanuts. Ward, transparently sincere and a former Rams international, did not enjoy his time as manager. "You had to ask the board for permission to stamp a letter," was his comment on a lack of ambition. Ward was, however, responsible for one of Derby's greatest signings when, in September, 1966, Kevin Hector arrived from Bradford Park Avenue for £40,000. He landed the man who was to smash Derby's appearances record and become only the second, after Steve Bloomer, to pass 200 goals for the club: not that Bloomer's 332 was ever in danger. As with many successful signings, plenty were eager to claim credit but Brian Clough was always unequivocal: "Tim Ward brought Kevin to Derby, nobody else."

Somehow, St Catherine's Society, Oxford, was persuaded to accept me to read English from 1957. The head of the college, known as the Censor, was Alan Bullock, famous as the author of a definitive biography of Hitler, and it was a source of regret that I never spoke to him in three years. Bullock was pressing on with plans for building a new college, Cats in my time being an administrative building which, because it was next to the police station in St Aldate's, was frequently mistaken for the morgue. It has to be confessed that my support for Derby flagged slightly in those years, in part because I was playing so often but also because London was so temptingly near in term time. There was, however, an important stage in my development because, for two of my three summers at Oxford, I worked as a holiday relief in the *Derby Telegraph* sports department. It would have been three but, in 1959, there was a National Graphical Association strike and employment was found in a Christmas cracker factory on Boulton Lane, right on the spot where my uncle once manufactured ice-cream. The sports department was enormous fun and gave me a taste for the profession. Cec Groundsell, who wrote for many years under the name of Mark Eaton, was the sports editor, Wilf Shaw covered the Rams, Brian Sparkes kept the production side going, although lathered in sweat at the end of every day, and there were two young men, compulsive gigglers like me, who would go far. George Edwards, from Matlock, was the Derby County correspondent in the early years of Clough and Taylor. After I joined full time, he became assistant editor and then moved to Swansea where, after an unduly long wait, he was appointed editor of the *South Wales Evening Post*. When he retired in 2002, the Swansea paper put on a terrific party for a man who boosted their circulation by following traditional ideals. Find the best story of the day and put it on the front page. It sounds obvious but so many editors ignore the essential path. Mike Carey, the other youngster, was the most gifted Derby journalist of my time, with an instinctive feel for words. He nursed ideas, hoping, for example, that he could see Vanburn Holder bowling to an in-form Peter Graves – a vin ordinaire against a Graves superiure. That never came to fruition but, after working for Raymonds' News Agency in Derby, Carey went on his own as a freelance and ultimately landed his ideal job as the *Daily Telegraph* cricket correspondent. It ended unhappily in a dispute, leading to Carey's resignation, which could have been handled better by both sides.

Having played and watched too much football, I emerged from Oxford with a moderate degree but was offered a teaching job by David Carr, whose brother Donald was Derbyshire's only England captain and was succeeded as the county secretary by Douglas Carr, the oldest of the three brothers. David, who taught me at Foremarke Hall, had been appointed joint-headmaster of Yarlet Hall, a preparatory school between Stone and Stafford. Would I go and teach English? David was one of the finest school-masters I ever met and was also a remarkable cricketer. He was wounded at Caen during World War Two and was alarmed to realise his bowling arm was out of action. He taught himself to bat one-handed, bowl some left-arm spin and flick the ball in as a fielder with his wrong hand, doing it all well enough to captain Derbyshire Second team as well as the Club and Ground. Will Taylor asked him to take a summer off to lead the Second team but David, then at the Repton Prep School, declined because of his teaching commitments. His overwhelming enthusiasm and love of the game made him an outstanding coach. It was a lovely life in a perfect setting, open country so near to the Potteries. There were some good men, dedicated teachers, and very few of the fly-by-nights that level can attract. The snag was that the pupils disappeared at 13, just when they were start-ing to prove some ability, and I found that hard to handle. One of my colleagues, Norman Ellis, was a keen follower of Wrexham and, at that time, lived opposite to the Racecourse. Through him, I became interested in the Welsh Cup and went to two Finals, one at Rhyl and another at

Llandudno Junction, home of Borough United. Newport County reached the Final against Borough and the League players went out to prod a disdainful toe into a heavily grassed pitch and look at the spectators, separated from the pitch only by a metal bar through concrete posts on three sides of the ground. Newport contrived to look snooty but lost over two legs to send Borough into the European Cup Winners' Cup, home games to be staged at Wrexham. Cups reach a conclusion around the same time and there could be no sharper contrast to Wembley or Hampden Park. Saturday was a working day at a boarding school but my half-day on a Monday was, at the time, Port Vale's midweek date. I went to Vale Park frequently, often by catching a train from Stone before changing to the splendid Burslem loop-line, and once saw Czechoslovakia there. They had World Cup qualifying matches in Scotland and the Republic of Ireland, so arranged to play Vale in between as part of their preparations. They took it seriously and did not flood the field with second-half substitutes, a practice that makes modern friendly internationals little short of fraudulent, especially given the cost of admission. Czechoslovakia were on the right lines because they qualified for Chile and reached the World Cup Final in Santiago, losing to Brazil.

Worthy as the Vale were, the great excitement in the Potteries was the return of Stanley Matthews to Stoke City in October, 1961, at the age of 46. Attendances were multiplied by four overnight and there was a banner with a rogue apostrophe to greet his second coming: 'Welcome back, Stan, thank's a million.' Tony Waddington, Stoke's affable and socially active manager, was on a winner because he brought in a stream of players who, but for the presence of Matthews, would have been called veterans. Before and after promotion, they included some of the most engaging performers of the time – Jimmy McIlroy, Jackie Mudie, Roy Vernon, Dennis Viollet, Peter Dobing, George Eastham. Add the more defensively inclined Wolverhampton Wanderers duo, Eddie Stuart and Eddie Clamp, and Waddington had a team to win promotion and maintain a First Division place. His signings had two things in common, they were winners and they could play. They were also canny professionals and it was often better to see them at the Victoria Ground than in away games. Waddington could be accused of short-term planning but fans want instant success and, when he died after several years of mellow retirement, scarves and flowers swamped the Victoria Ground. Stoke people knew Waddington gave them some wonderful entertainment. By contrast, it was a plain time at the Baseball Ground, with little suggestion that Derby would leave the Second Division: if they did, it would certainly not be upwards. The board was dimly unambitious, with tight controls on managers, so we took consolation in players who had a spark. Some offered enduring quality, like Geoff Barrowcliffe with his elegant defending or Tommy Powell with his control. Jack Parry on his way to setting a club record for appearances, was by then a midfield player, his attacking spark dulled by the serious injury in 1956. Harry Storer signed Bill Curry, a centre-forward with style and swagger. Curry was not always the hardest worker but 76 goals in 164 games prove his effectiveness and eye for the target.

In 1963, I moved to an even more attractive setting, accepting Guy Willatt's offer to teach at Heversham Grammar School on the edge of the Lake District. On the night before the interview, I was offered a room that looked out over the estuary towards Morecambe Bay but, when the job became reality, the only view was of the headmaster's greenhouse: Willatt remained a tactician. In those days, the M6 ended at Carnforth, and on summer weekends it was possible to savour the endless queue of traffic waiting to go through the traffic lights at Milnthorpe. There is the same feeling of malicious satisfaction now when cars are hopelessly clogged on the other side of a motorway. This change meant my viewing habits altered. The North Lancashire clubs were easily accessible and it took only 90 minutes to reach Manchester or Liverpool. Long before the Taylor Report and all-seater stadia, the sole qualification for getting in was to arrive early enough. When Liverpool played Internazionale in a European Cup semi-final in 1965, I dumped my books in Heversham as soon as the bell sounded. It was reasonably easy to park and there were few on the way to Anfield. I realised why when I pressed into what was then a terrace in front of the main stand: Anfield was heaving and not many would have gained admission after me. That was a magical night. Two injured players, Gerry Byrne and Gordon Milne, carried round the FA Cup, the first time Liverpool had ever won it. Then Inter were hounded and hammered 3-1. After Derby County beat Real Madrid at the Baseball Ground in the European Cup, I sought a word with Bill Shankly, who was there as a spectator, and asked how it compared with Liverpool's great nights. "I was like the time we beat Inter Milan 3-1," Shankly replied. "It should have been 4-1 but Chrissie Lawler had a perfectly good goal disallowed." Ten years on and the decision still rankled with Shankly. In 1967-68, I saw all Manchester United's home matches on their way to the European Cup Final. My first trip to Old Trafford was to see United play Red Star Belgrade in January, 1958, one of a handful of glimpses of the Busby Babes. The power of Duncan Edwards, the style of Tommy Taylor at centre-forward, the Manchester impudence of Eddie Colman at wing-half, the mature cool of Roger Byrne at left-back are the memories. They were, too, a loved side. Supporters of opposing clubs were prepared to enjoy that United team, well before the days of compulsory hatred and witless jeering. United survived magnificently in the second leg in Belgrade but their world ended with the Munich air crash on the way home. I heard of it as I was coming out of the Bodleian Library in Oxford and the country was stunned. So 1967-68 was the chance to put the record straight and we knew they would do it after they followed a 1-0 home win over Real Madrid with a 3-3 draw in the Bernabeu Stadium, helped by a rare goal from Billy Foulkes.

The Final against Benfica was at Wembley and might never have gone into extra-time. Eusebio was through and, instead of placing his shot, tried to lift the net off its moorings. Alex Stepney managed to cling on and United ran away with the game in the extra half-hour. Busby was fulfilled and, for the first time, I went over a hill on the M1 to see three lines of taillights stretching ahead. Now that is the scene every day of the week. Heversham did not revolve entirely around football trips, because there was a boarding house to run, boys wanting exam qualifications and, perhaps most time consuming, a Cadet Force to organise. I enjoyed it and one of the proudest moments came when every member of my B stream passed English Language at O level: we had beaten the examining board.

Guy Willatt left in 1966 to become headmaster of Pocklington School in Yorkshire and I entered an unsettled period. I went for one interview at a school in Cleethorpes and was told I could have the job if I taught Latin: that would have been manifestly unfair to the pupils. I fled from another school in Bristol, having summed up the headmaster and his staff, but took a job in Widnes. It was an error, rectified after one term by becoming senior English master at Richmond School in Yorkshire. It was in another attractive setting, overlooked by Richmond Castle and sitting above the River Swale. At last free of boarding house commitments, I rented a flat in Marske Hall, an 18th-century country house in the tiny Swaledale village. From my kitchen window, I could see into the house across Marske Beck, just a glimpse of a room where the walls were entirely covered by books. It was the retirement home of Sir Rupert Hart-Davis, the publisher. Swaledale is one of the most peaceful places in the world and I retained the flat, tempted by the restorative properties of the area, for the next 10 years.

By this stage, my Saturdays were free and Derby County were on the move. Tim Ward's contract was not renewed in 1967 and, thanks to a recommendation from Len Shackleton, Brian Clough was appointed. He handled the negotiations in his own way and one director later said: "We had the impression he was interviewing us, rather than the other way round." As, indeed, he was and had already accepted the job when he pointed out that Peter Taylor would be accompanying him. One of the first questions Clough asked George Edwards, then covering the club for the *Derby Telegraph*, was: "What are your edition times?" The new manager had plenty to say and, because he said it so well, national papers soon realised there were stories to be had around the Baseball Ground. There was no instant improvement and Derby dropped a place in the Second Division under the new regime, to 18th. At the same time, supporters quickly realised that a better class of player was coming through the door. The first three signings under Clough and Taylor were John O'Hare, Roy McFarland and Alan Hinton. For a total outlay of less than £75,000, Derby had three players who, between them, made 1,154 appearances and scored 212 goals. Clough knew O'Hare from his days as Sunderland Youth coach:

when Clough and Taylor were in charge at Hartlepools United, they saw the young McFarland in the Tranmere Rovers side: Hinton was nearer their new home, having a thin time in a struggling Nottingham Forest side. Forest committee men were overhead to say Derby would soon be asking for their money back but Clough and Taylor merely wanted a few more of Forest's players. McFarland's ability at centre-half was soon appreciated but acceptance was slower for the other two. O'Hare had no pace and, despite his broad shoulders, was not a battering ram at centre-forward. What he could do, which is why other players had so much admiration, was make himself available for a pass, hold the ball when it came and survive close attention from defenders not too worried if they took the man first. And he scored his share of goals. Hinton was never one to get stuck in, nor did Clough and Taylor particularly want him to, although there were occasional suggestions that he might at least stand in the way of opponents. He was their outlet on the left, to hold the ball and deliver it with the immaculate technique he learned from a former England winger, Jimmy Mullen, when he was a junior with Wolverhampton Wanderers. Hinton had two great feet, he measured centres and there were some memorably explosive goals. When Clough and Taylor rejoined forces with Nottingham Forest, the shape of the team was instantly familiar to those who had watched Derby: for Hinton, read John Robertson. The pass out to the left bought time, allowed other to regroup and finally produced the main danger.

If O'Hare and Hinton struggled for due recognition, John McGovern never fully achieved it, either with Derby or Forest. And this is a man who won Championships with both clubs, League Cups with Forest and twice raised the European Cup as Forest captain. McGovern was first seen as a Grammar School boy in Hartlepool. "We held trials for kids," said Taylor. "Bring your own soap and towels. After half-an-hour, I told Brian to have the gates locked. We didn't want John to leave before he signed a schoolboy form." McGovern was 18 when he followed Clough and Taylor to Derby for £7,500 but he had an awkward running style. There was nothing flamboyant about his game: he oiled the wheels in midfield, winning or accepting the ball and moving it on quickly. He needed strength of character to overcome public suspicion but had that in abundance. "He's like Alan Hinton," said Taylor. "People won't realise how good they are until they're no longer playing for us." Although Clough and Taylor were convinced that progress was made in 1967-68, they were also aware of the need for extra ingredients to pull everything together, like experience and character.

The first move electrified Derby. One summer day in 1968, Clough drove to White Hart Lane with permission to approach Dave Mackay. Although Bill Nicholson, the most successful of all Tottenham Hotspur managers, warned it would be a waste of time because Mackay was expected to rejoin his first club, Heart of Midlothian, Clough was determined to see it through. Mackay won everything with Hearts at the start of his career before Nicholson signed him in 1959. He was the driving force in midfield when, in 1960-61, Spurs became the first 20th century team to win the League and Cup double. Other players in that side happily acknowledged that Dave was the key to that success and he was in two more Cup-winning sides, as well as breaking his left leg twice. Somehow, Clough persuaded him to join Derby and my reaction was probably echoed by many supporters: "That's marvellous but I'll only fully believe it when I see him run out at the Baseball Ground." There he was, chest first, for a pre-season friendly against St Johnstone: Dave Mackay of Derby County. The midfield warrior had a new role, to play at the back and organise an essentially young defence around him – Ron Webster, Roy McFarland and John Robson. For three years, it was a master-class as Mackay cajoled, barked and demonstrated the range of his skill. He was a wonderful kicker of the ball, short, long, volleys, half-volleys, the lot. As with Bobby Charlton, it was worth paying the money to see Mackay warming up before matches but, more than anything else, he was a leader, on and off the field.

Even with Mackay in the side, there was a spluttering start to 1968-69, three draws and two defeats in the first five games. Clough and Taylor knew who they wanted and, finally, £60,000 persuaded Sheffield United to sell Willie Carlin, a spiky Liverpudlian nurtured in the lower divisions by Halifax Town and Carlisle United after leaving Anfield. Carlin was intensely competitive and would not tolerate any lapse in standards, apart from being an expert at winding up opponents. He made his debut in a midweek draw with Hull City and three days later, Alan Durban was restored to the side. The blend was right and Derby lost only three League games after August. By the time they completed the season with a club record nine consecutive victories, the opposition was scattered and one long celebration culminated in a 5-0 defeat of Bristol City, sparked by Durban's hat-trick. Derby were back in Division One for the first time since 1953 and an exile of 16 often dispiriting years was behind them. As crowds rose, it was no longer possible to amble in and pick a spot. Early arrival and greater knowledge were required but even when the terraces were heaving, there was a haven at the Normanton End. On the corner nearest the Popular Side, the terracing rose to a small peak and it was always possible to stand there in reasonable comfort. Even so, better accommodation was needed for the First Division and the Ley Stand was built in the summer of 1969, the first significant development since the construction of the Normanton Stand in 1935. Such was the demand that priority was given to those prepared to buy season tickets for two years and these were quickly taken. I was among them so, for the first time in my life, the terraces were deserted in favour of a regular seat.

It was a wonderful time to be following Derby County because of the excitement and pride that gripped the town, as it then was. We had always thought the Rams ought to be in the First Division, on grounds of history and tradition, but, for so many years, there was no chance that the dream would become reality. Clough and Taylor not only achieved promotion with the flourish produced by an obviously gifted team, they had the Rams sitting at the top of the table in mid-September. George Edwards remembers Clough in the coach outside St James' Park, unable to take his eyes off the *Newcastle Pink* after McFarland's goal lifted Derby to first place. A week later, Mackay led his team to a 5-0 victory over Tottenham Hotspur in front of a record 41,826 at the Baseball Ground. They did not suffer defeat until the 12th game, when they went down to Sheffield Wednesday at Hillsborough, and although the season levelled out, Derby finished fourth, playing some of the most attractive football in the land. Leeds

United, Liverpool and Everton, all beaten at the Baseball Ground, finished ahead of them. There was another 40,000 attendance for the visit of Leeds at the end of March, 1970, and there was a collective gasp when their team was read out. Don Revie, in the middle of a fixture tangle because of progress to the FA Cup Final and a European Cup semi-final against Celtic, picked his Reserves. If the crowd felt let down, they were cheered by a 4-1 victory and fourth place took them into Europe: or so we thought. Not for the first time in the Derby story, there was an FA commission lying in wait. The main crime was to pay Mackay, outside the terms of his contract, for brief articles in the club programme but the administration was exposed by the galloping success. There was ticket money all over the offices and the staff could not cope. Derby were fined and, more deflating for management, players and fans, deprived of the European place they earned. The first solution was to appoint Stuart Webb, previously assistant at Preston North End, as secretary. He was to figure prominently in the next 30 years in a variety of roles, including chairman, but for all their disappointment, supporters knew they had a tremendous team, including their first £100,000 signing, Terry Hennessey from Nottingham Forest. A feeling persisted that the best days were ahead and not much time was needed to prove it.

LISTENING TO CLOUGH

THE half-term break from Richmond School in summer, 1970, was an opportunity to watch some cricket at Queen's Park and, as it turned out, change the direction of my life. During a social visit to the Press box at the lunch interval, I was told that David Moore, who then covered cricket for the *Derby Evening Telegraph*, was about to join Derby County as programme editor. He encouraged me to put in for the vacancy, as did Mike Carey and Neil Hallam, an influential freelance who ran the sport for Raymonds News Agency in Derby. The previous autumn, when Carey found himself needing to be in two places at once for the *Guardian*, I fielded substitute for him at a Wolverhampton Wanderers evening game. There was some dabbling in the North-East, both for the *Guardian* and, thanks to the kindness of Alan Hughes, *Goal*, a weekly magazine. The atmosphere of Press boxes was fascinating, something to which the increasing penetration by outsiders now bears witness, and congenial. Having felt something of an intruder while involved as an occasional dabbler, it was time to take the step on a regular basis and there was another factor to take into account. As part of Government policy, Richmond School was moving towards comprehensive status and while that would mean increased pay as the potential senior English master, I was far from sure that it would suit my idea of teaching: the remedial class may not have been the right environment.

Watching cricket professionally promised to be a pleasant way of life but the scale was heavily tilted by Brian Clough and what he was creating at the Baseball Ground. The afternoon's cricket rather escaped me but, by the time I went home, the decision was taken. A telephone call to George Edwards led to a meeting at a pub in Whatstandwell, quickly followed by an interview with the editor, John Low. There was a 20 per cent drop in salary but the job was fixed, to start as soon as the summer term at Richmond was over. My exam forms were in good shape for their joust with the Northern Board but the second year sixth, due to sit A levels in 1971, obviously felt they were being abandoned. There is a degree of pot luck in schools because in Westmorland, results suggested that chemistry was a fiendishly difficult course while physics presented few problems: in North Yorkshire, exactly the opposite obtained, so everything depends on the quality of individual teachers. As it happened, the Richmond students fared well under my successor and it is not practical to have too much of a conscience about a career move. All was set for the end of July, 1970, with Nottinghamshire at Worksop in the John Player League and at Trent Bridge in the Championship as the opening assignment. My first day was the Sunday but I went to Trent Bridge the day before to see how the Championship game was shaping, sitting out in the crowd at my own expense. That error was not repeated, as I proved a quick learner on maximising expenses claims. On the Monday, which was hit by rain, several of the Derbyshire players wandered across to inspect their new reporter. It was an obvious advantage to know them all by sight and to have watched them play but they were very welcoming. On away trips in the 1970s and 1980s, they always made sure there was a casual invitation to eat with them in an evening or chat round a bar. They did not leave people to their own devices and, in those days, there was far more talk about the game, so it was easier to learn how the players saw it in the middle. It was soon apparent there was little point in discussing dismissals. After being caught behind in the Yorkshire game one year, Mike Page claimed he missed the ball by six inches: Richard Hutton, the bowler I knew from his time at Repton School, maintained he had half-a-bat on it. It was the old 'look in the book' solution and umpires remain the best, as well as an extremely congenial, source of informed opinion. They have an unrivalled view of events and it is ludicrous that selectors do not consult them more often. At some time in the mid-1990s, I asked Kenny Palmer over a beer outside the St Lawrence Ground in Canterbury when was the last time he had his brains picked about the merits of possible England players. It had not happened for more than a decade, in the preparations for Mike Gatting's tour to Australia.

Before settling into the job, one further hurdle appeared. The local branch of the National Union of Journalists took the hump about somebody strolling in from a classroom and rejected my application to join. The voting was 3-2 against, so not many turned up to discuss this vital issue, and the editor told me not to worry. It was all sorted out eventually and, as a member, I took part in the NUJ's ill-conceived provincial strike of 1978-79. As I stood aimlessly on a picket line outside the back entrance of the *Evening Telegraph*, one passer-by accused me of being a Communist: he was a touch wide of the mark but various full-time union officials lectured us from time to time about the 'bosses' and the 'fat Christmas editions' – which we had totally failed to affect. It is hard to imagine a strike being run more ineptly and it took years to catch up with the money lost on wages. Relations with individual members of the National Graphical Association, the print union, were temporarily soured, perhaps because they regarded striking as their prerogative.

I had met Brian Clough once, in the promotion season, when I went from North Yorkshire to see Derby at Carlisle. George Edwards fixed a ticket for me and took me back to the hotel afterwards. I thanked Clough for the ticket and ventured that it had been cold in the stand. "It would have been a bloody sight colder on the terraces," he said, an excellent response for my anecdotal purposes. For the most part, I was wise enough to listen, both then and when it was my job to do so. Clough and Peter Taylor made up a unique well of knowledge about the game, so it would have been criminal to squander such an opportunity to learn. Up to my retirement, I remained conscious of how many thousands in Derby would cherish such access to management and players: there was a responsibility to readers, so the opportunities had to be used for their benefit. My brief, which suited perfectly, was to help Edwards with Derby County as well as covering Derbyshire. The 1970-71 season, starting a trail that was to last almost 32 years, kicked off at Stamford Bridge, where Derby lost 2-1 to Chelsea, and I stayed in London for another three days to watch Derbyshire play Essex at Leyton, an unappealing ground given historical significance by the 555 opening partnership between Percy Holmes and Herbert Sutcliffe for Yorkshire in 1932.

The immediate fascination lay at the Baseball Ground, as Clough and Taylor were in the process of building not only a team but a club. They had been friends of Harry Storer, under whom Taylor played at Coventry City. Storer wanted to sign Clough before he broke into the Middlesbrough team and, although nothing came of it, a lasting bond was formed. They made sure his widow had a seat whenever she wanted to see Derby but, in their blunter moments, reflected that Storer failed at the Baseball Ground. He did the first job, winning promotion from Division Three North, but was unable to take it on from there. The board of the time was hardly brimming with ambition, as Tim Ward discovered in his five years as manager. The Rams were cast as a middle-ranking Second Division club, which was why I goggled at my morning paper in Westmorland when it carried news that Kevin Hector had signed from Bradford for £40,000. Derby simply didn't shell out money at that level but Ward, acutely conscious that the fans needed a star, somehow persuaded the board that it was a good deal. Hector was 21 when he joined Derby but already had a century of League goals for Bradford, 113 in 176 games, and the surprise was that none of the bigger clubs was prepared to invest in such obvious potential. Hector was the jewel left for Clough and Taylor but there were others. Ron Webster signed as a professional in 1960, when Storer was in charge, and set out as a wing-half. He reached the heights for Derby at right-back, the local boy who survived and contributed to the success. Other players came to feel that Webster was the best natural defender at the club because he had a great eye for developing danger and would find the right position to deal with it. Like many home-grown players in successful clubs, he was at once enormously popular and underestimated: those who grow up through the ranks often find themselves taken for granted. Clough and Taylor had a goalkeeper on the premises but it took time for them to appreciate Colin Boulton, like Ward a native of Cheltenham. In their first season, they stuck with Reg Matthews, tough, almost absurdly brave but coming towards the end of a fine career. Then they bought Les Green, who played under them at Hartlepools United, from Rochdale. Green was small but agile and, his greatest recommendation to the management, vocally skilled organising a defence. His natural humour was good for the team and he appeared in 129 consecutive games before his form wobbled. He was dropped after a 4-4 draw against Manchester United on Boxing Day, 1970, and never regained his place. Just how well Boulton accepted the opportunity is illustrated by the fact that he alone appeared in all 84 games across Derby's two Championship seasons, during which he made remarkably few mistakes. Peter Daniel, a product of Ward's thorough screening of local talent, had to wait even longer for recognition, when Roy McFarland's Achilles tendon injury in 1974 let him in as Colin Todd's partner in the second Championship. Daniel emerged as Player of the Year, although it was suggested the supporters' votes were level and Todd graciously stepped aside. Ward's other legacy was Alan Durban, a crafty player he signed from Cardiff City. He had no pace but an acute football brain which, when he slotted into midfield, guided his passing and took him to the right place as a late arriver in penalty areas. The typical Durban goal trundled over the line but there were 112 of them for Derby. He began by forming a dangerous inside-forward partnership with Eddie Thomas but reached the heights in midfield.

Taylor always prided himself on the speed with which he assessed players and a few lasted longer than might have been the case because some of the new signings were ineligible for the run to the semi-finals of the 1967-68 League Cup. That was essential in creating enthusiasm, because Second Division results were no better than in Ward's final year. Success in either Cup was then a rarity but the draw was kind. They beat Hartlepools and Birmingham City, attracted a record crowd to Sincil Bank for a replay victory over Lincoln City and reached the last four with an extraordinary 5-4 win over Darlington at the Baseball Ground. They lost to Leeds United, about to win their first major trophy under Don Revie, over two legs but the seven matches showed how eagerly the Derby public would respond to success. Clough and Taylor almost established a monopoly on the League Cup when they were together with Nottingham Forest: they simply wanted to win every competition, at all levels. Their first move was to bring in John O'Hare from Sunderland, soon to be followed by Roy McFarland and Alan Hinton. Pat Wright, a full-back from Shrewsbury Town, and Richie Barker, an experienced non-League striker who arrived from Burton Albion, turned out to be shorter-term investments, as did Arthur Stewart, a Northern Ireland international wing-half from Glentoran. They were always ready to look outside the League, so Jim Walker was signed from Northwich Victoria. At the end of that first season, there was a significant debut when John Robson, spotted by Taylor when playing for Birtley in the North-East, set out at the age of 17.

It was always clear that those on the staff would go if Clough and Taylor could find better players. They even said that about McFarland and had a long look at Dave Watson: "If we can see a better centre-half than McFarland, then we want him at Derby," was the refrain but they never discovered one. A pattern began to emerge in the first season and support made it clear what Derby could achieve but there was a need to raise the level of ability. Dave Mackay was the ideal solution, quality and experience to guide young players, a natural leader with a record that could not fail to excite supporters. "Signing David Mackay was the best day's work I ever did," Clough said hundreds of times. Not only did Mackay lead Derby out of the Second Division as joint Footballer of the Year, tied with Manchester City veteran Tony Book, but gave them two terrific years in the First. He signed off in 1970-71 with a full house of 42 League games, fulfilling an ambition with the first ever-present season of his career. Mackay hastened the development of other players in two ways. First, he was so good that anybody with talent could not fail to learn and the other point was that his status in the game made him the focus of attention, for supporters as well as Press, so that the rest had the comfort of maturing in his shadow. It was not that Mackay sought attention: he compelled it through his presence and gave the fans boasting rights as they grabbed the reflected glory.

Once Willie Carlin arrived from Sheffield United for the fifth game of the 1968-69 season, Clough and Taylor had a team good enough not only to surge through the Second Division but to play in the First. An earlier attempt to sign Carlin from Carlisle United landed them with an accusation of tapping-up, the classic illegal approach, when Tim Ward, then in charge at Brunton Park, complained. They suggested a journalist friend, Doug Weatherall, should sow a few seeds but, when asked to clarify the position, the *Daily Mail's* man in the North-East pointed out that Carlisle also came into his patch, so he was merely interviewing the player. After leaving Liverpool, Carlin had some tough times with Halifax where, as he said, crowds were small enough for him to pick out individuals giving him stick. When he was at Carlisle, he bumped into one referee a couple of hours before kick-off and received his first warning of the day: "I don't want any trouble from you this time." Near the end of a Carlisle victory at the Baseball Ground, Carlin ran the ball into the corners to eat up time and was chased off at the end by an enraged Reg Matthews, while rubbing thumb against fingers to indicate who had the win bonus. He was a competitor and, having been released by Liverpool at the start of his career, was possessed by an unquenchable thirst for success.

The right mixture of talents was fundamental to Taylor's belief and Derby had it once Carlin arrived. It was also clear that, although the basis for success was there, Clough and Taylor would never be content with it because there were always players who could bring about improvement. The initial overhaul was complete, so their signings could be more selective and made in their own time, often around February to give final impetus to a season while keeping an eye on the following August. The arrival of Frank Wignall, who won two England caps with Nottingham Forest and was then with Wolverhampton Wanderers, in February, 1969, was more of an insurance policy. By then, promotion was looming but Wignall gave cover and competition to the forwards, not that John O'Hare and Kevin Hector missed many games. Famously, Clough dropped Hector for a match against Nottingham Forest at the City Ground in March, 1970. It was the only time Hector was absent all season but Wignall looked after the formidable Sammy Chapman, catching him on the ankle without breaking stride. Wignall was what Ron Atkinson would call the reducer on that occasion and tested the John McGrath theory – 'Let's see how fast he can limp.' A year after Wignall's arrival, the stakes were raised sharply when Terry Hennessey became Derby's first £100,000 player. In four-and-a-half years with Nottingham Forest, Hennessey became king of the City Ground but, when he was out through injury in 1969-70, Liam O'Kane stood in with considerable success. Clough and Taylor watched the situation, delighted with every good Forest result because they felt in would make it easier to land their man. When they moved in, Forest agreed to sell, although they later became more reluctant to deal when Derby pursued Ian Storey-Moore and Henry Newton. Hennessey, a Welsh international who began his career with Birmingham City, was a tremendous player, either in defence or midfield, and easily picked out through his bald head. He was seen as a natural successor to Mackay who, typically, showed no inclination to give way: if Hennessey wanted that particular shirt, he would have to earn it by demonstrating he could do a better job. As it turned out, Derby seldom saw the best of Hennessey as he was constantly troubled by injuries stemming from a pre-season match against Port Vale, first knee, then Achilles tendon. There was a tantalising glimpse of how influential he could have been when he defended magnificently against Benfica in the Estadio da Luz during Derby's first European Cup venture. Although they held a 3-0 lead from the first leg, the Rams had to work hard for a 0-0, with Colin Boulton also having one of his finest games. Hennessey's top-level career ended at Derby and, after non-League management, he turned to coaching in the United States and Australia.

A year after promotion, Derby finished fourth in the First Division but administrative problems denied them a place in the UEFA Cup. They had to make do with the Watney Cup, a pre-season tournament for the highest scorers and, having the main prize denied, set about winning it. After beating Fulham at Craven Cottage and Sheffield United at home, they attracted 32,049 to the Baseball Ground for a 4-1 victory over Manchester United in the Final. The essential was to sort out the club's administration and, in June, 1970, they appointed Stuart Webb as secretary. He had been assistant to John Howarth at Preston North End, so had a proper apprenticeship, and proved to be one of the best in the business. It was not always easy because Clough liked to be involved in every aspect of Derby's affairs and Webb had to mark out his territory. Over the years, he went through the card as secretary, general secretary, the subject of a long, costly and ultimately unproductive police investigation, director, chairman and director again. The common thread was that Derby had infinitely more success when he was involved than they did with him on the outside. Webb also played a part in the next signing, having seen at close quarters the way Archie Gemmill developed in three years since joining Preston from St Mirren. Clough and Taylor were keen to inject some pace into their midfield and Webb suggested that Gemmill could be the answer. This became one of the classic Clough deals, when he refused to go home without a signature on the transfer form. They did that with Roy McFarland after a night match at Tranmere, reaching agreement with Dave Russell before going to McFarland's home in Liverpool. Clough and Taylor persuaded McFarland's parents that a move to Derby was the right thing before England's future centre-half came downstairs in his pyjamas. Clough stayed the night with the Gemmills, because he knew that Everton were also keen and had a valuable ally in Alan Ball senior. With Clough's charm and persuasive qualities at full power, Gemmill agreed to sign in September, 1970, embarking on a career that brought him three Championship medals and 43 Scottish caps. He even managed to emerge from Scotland's gruesome campaign in the 1978 World Cup finals in Argentina with his reputation not only intact but enhanced after his classic goal against Holland. The signing hastened the end of Carlin, who went to Leicester City the following month. Just as Clough and Taylor personified welcoming eagerness when they wanted to bring in a player, so they were often dismissively curt when they shifted one out. Carlin was on the end of a 'get down to the ground, we're selling you' telephone call and duly found himself moving down the road. It was of a piece with, particularly, Taylor's philosophy: once they decided to do something, the best way was to sort it out and move on. If that was best for the club, there was no time to lose, no point in hanging about. When Wignall left for Mansfield Town three months into the first Championship season, Clough urged him to play for as long as possible: "Once you stop, there is nothing to replace it," said Clough and in that sentence came an echo of his own frustration about an early retirement, forced on him by a severe knee injury. Clough's record for Middlesbrough was phenomenal, 267 goals in 296 League and Cup games. When he told Taylor he was about to join Sunderland, his future partner was straight round to his bookmaker to lay money on Clough's goals earning promotion at Roker Park. The injury occurred against Bury, when goalkeeper Chris Harker dived out at Clough's feet on a frosty pitch and wrecked his knee ligaments. Former Newcastle United centre-half Bob Stokoe, at Bury winding down his career, became a life-long enemy by standing over Clough and accusing him of making a fuss about nothing. Although Clough tried to return in the First Division, his knee could not cope and when he walked around the Baseball Ground in shorts, the massive operation scars were clearly visible. Carlin did a great job for Derby, signing for a Second Division club and leaving one making enough of an impact in the First for ninth place in 1970-71 to be regarded as a disappointment. Clough and Taylor had one more card to play that season and, as Derby shuddered through the Rolls-Royce crisis, it proved to be a winner. Sunderland were ready to sell Colin Todd who, at 22, was widely regarded as the best young defender in England and was, of course, no stranger to Clough, a former Youth coach at Roker. There were rumours that Derby were in the frame but Clough dismissed them. "We can't afford him," he said, shortly before getting into his car to drive to the North-East and negotiate with Alan Brown. The following day, in front of the same audience, Clough introduced Todd, signed for £170,000. I asked where Todd would play in Derby's next game at Blackpool and no question could have suited Clough better. "He might not get a game," he said. "He might sit next to me on the bench and watch how we play." That is exactly what happened and there was a reminder eight years later when Trevor Francis joined Nottingham Forest (another February signing) as the first £1m player and was promptly named in the A team. That rebounded slightly, because Francis was not properly registered for that competition, but Clough seldom missed a chance to make his point. Sam Longson was away on holiday when the Todd deal was completed and received a cable to inform him, with the rider 'Please send more money.' At that time, Longson was playing the part of the indulgent patron, without risking much of his own money, and adopted a paternal attitude towards Clough. Taylor, with greater experience of football's ways, used to beg his friend not to be so close to the chairman or, indeed, any director. Although nobody knew it, Longson still had a Championship coming to crown his period in office – and chairmen are entitled to be judged by results – but when the relationship soured, the in-fighting was bitter. Taylor was right in his feeling that all directors should be kept at arm's length. It is essential for managers to have good working relationships with their boards but anything more personal becomes dangerous ground.

It was hard for Longson to be anything other than pleased by the acquisition of Todd, who was so clearly a player to strengthen any team. It was obvious where Todd would play but the place next to Roy McFarland was not available until Dave Mackay completed his final season. Swindon Town wanted Mackay, initially as a player but with an eye on management, so the final game of the season, at home to West Bromwich Albion, was identified as his farewell. There was nothing at stake but there were 33,661 in the Baseball Ground to say goodbye to a master player who gave Derby the final years of a great career. He left as he had arrived and always played, with a swagger. There was nothing sentimental about it, because Mackay knew his job at Derby was done, but there was a feeling of immense gratitude. Supporters were happy to have seen three years of Mackay, during which time he helped to give the club a new identity and enhanced status. For their part, Clough and Taylor offered him an unexpected last fling at the top, so it was a perfect signing. Many others tried to reproduce it and several talented veterans changed clubs and found themselves expected 'to do a Dave Mackay'. Not one managed to achieve the same impact. For a start, few ever matched the ingredients that made Mackay such a force and nor did they find such a good set of circumstances, intelligent management, promising young players and supporters desperate to be involved in an overdue revival. Todd made half-a-dozen of his appearances at right-back, with enough poise to suggest it was his natural position. One tackle at Old Trafford was startling as Todd, head-on, met the ball with perfect timing backed by the strength of his legs and body. The Manchester United player, Paul Edwards, was left shuddering, although there was no semblance of a foul. Todd's quality was so evident that it made saying goodbye to Mackay that much easier: the baton was passed on.

The other important change came at the turn of the year, after Les Green had a bad time in the 4-4 draw with Manchester United on Boxing Day. Colin Boulton, who took over in goal, was 25 and, in more than five seasons since Tim Ward signed him, mustered only 26 appearances as deputy to Reg Matthews and then Green. This was a marvellous opportunity to forge a career in a developing team and Boulton was ready for it. The jersey was more obviously his the following August, when Green went to play for Durban City in South Africa and, a few weeks later, the 17-year-old Graham Moseley was signed from Blackburn Rovers to learn his trade in the Reserves. The absence of transfer activity in the summer suggested Clough and Taylor were happy with their resources. As Derbyshire stumbled through a dismal 1971 season, finishing at the bottom of the County Championship with only one victory, at Blackheath over a Kent side weakened by Test calls, reflecting on the Rams' prospects helped to relieve the gloom. There was reason to be cheerful but I don't think many, even inside the manager's office, were ready to bet heavily on the title. History can limit expectations and, in the 83 years since Derby were original members of the League, their best was second position on three occasions, in 1895-96, 1929-30 and 1935-36, the last two under George Jobey. They reached three FA Cup Finals in the space of six years, 1898, 1899 and 1903, but their only success was the 1946 Wembley win over Charlton Athletic. Derby were known as a good club, if liable to land in trouble with the authorities, but one just below the aristocracy. As always, big cities provided most of the winners and Leeds United, under Don Revie, had the most talented side. Their trouble was that they were so keen to find an edge and extra advantage they often ended by cheating themselves. Roy McFarland maintains Leeds of that era were the best club team he encountered but they were less good at winning friends and should have picked up more trophies. Arsenal won the League and Cup double in 1970-71, settled almost as Charlie George lay on the Wembley turf celebrating his wonderful goal against Liverpool. On either side of Stanley Park, Liverpool and Everton, Bill Shankly and Harry Catterick, were powerful teams at big clubs. The Rams had to upset the natural order if they were to muscle in but we had genuine hopes they would present a challenge and, in the process, provide ample entertainment.

Finding a blend was one of Taylor's obsessions and, to him, it was the supreme test of management, best achieved by sticking to his other prime requirements, keeping clean sheets, still football speak for not conceding goals, and having a strong spine from goalkeeper to centre-forward. Supreme judgement and a touch of fortune is required to make all the pieces fit but Clough and Taylor worked with one mind. They tried to integrate character as well as skill, so that they had a group of players who would not let them down at moments of crisis. It was said that they ruled by fear and it is true that players were wary of them. As Martin O'Neill, intelligent enough to take in and use what he saw to build an excellent career in management, once said of Clough: "He can make you feel desperate for his approval." There was probably an element of apprehension but that is not enough on its own. It was more personality that created respect, coupled with the fact that so many of their decisions proved to be absolutely right. As Durban once said: "There are not too many complaints about somebody who doubles your wages." On occasions, they were cruel but they created terrific teams for Derby and Nottingham Forest, clubs that had never won the Championship before and, in the light of the change in football finances, are unlikely ever to repeat the feat. Two sets of supporters, separated by barely 20 miles, lived through days they will never see again. At least Clough reached retirement with Forest, even if it was marked by his first relegation. Derby cut him and Taylor off in their peak years, so everything that was savoured at the City Ground could have taken place up Shaftesbury Crescent. There was no hint of the turmoil to come when, in Spring, 1971, I embarked on my first full cricket season. Although I had watched cricket for many years and occasionally played with a marked lack of impact, travelling to all the away games was a new experience. Championship matches were over three days for most of my working life, starting on Wednesdays and Saturdays with a John Player

League game on Sunday, so it was easy to slip into a comfortable rhythm. There was little in the way of time off but that was never a problem, in part because Mike Carey, who always packed his Scrabble board, was a congenial travelling companion for several years until he moved on to greater things. We needed a sense of humour in the 1971 season, because both the weather and Derbyshire were poor. Ian Buxton, who did well in his first year as captain, found much the same team floundering at the foot of the table because Derbyshire's traditional strength, seam bowling, was unusually weak. Alan Ward and Bob Taylor went to Australia in 1970-71 but Ward had to return early because of injury. When Ward first played in 1966, England as well as Derbyshire welcomed the emergence of a genuinely fast bowler. Derbyshire tried to look after him while his strength developed but, in the end, injuries were a constant problem. So many previews to seasons contained the inescapable proviso: 'if Ward remains fit...'. Sadly, he was never strong enough to make a mark at Test level, although he played for England five times. He had a fine, high action but, with tall fast bowlers, there is an inbuilt risk of strains and pulls. Perhaps Ward had too gentle a personality, possibly ambition did not burn fiercely enough but by the time he moved to Leicestershire, his was already a career that did not fulfil the early promise. Taylor's did and, for 24 years, no Derbyshire summer was without merit because it offered a chance to see him keep wicket. For many years, he was a permanent number two at Test level, kept in the shadows by Alan Knott's consistency and superior batting. We used to discuss the respective merits of Knott and Taylor behind the stumps but there was very little in it and, anyway, the central action of cricket is a considerable distance from spectators. The key decisions, whether a catch was put down or how thick an edge was caught standing up, involved guesswork or a quiet inquiry at the end of the innings. Knott's decision to join Kerry Packer's World Series, an attempt to bust an Australian television monopoly that was to have a huge influence on the game's future development, gave Taylor a chance to play for England after his one earlier appearance. He ended with 57 Tests as well as the record, 1,649, for most dismissals in first-class cricket.

It is hard to imagine Taylor will ever be dislodged from that peak and he deserves the honour. 'Immaculate' was the word most often attached to him and was fair in everything he did. Taylor was a perfectionist and a model as a professional sportsman. There was great respect for the game in the way he set out to master his craft and he remains the most courteous of men. Underneath that lay a steel core of determination which may have started to appear when, as a boy, he practised so assiduously on Stoke City's car park but a combination of virtues over many years made his final season almost a royal progress around the counties. In fact, 1971 was not one of Taylor's best years because he broke a finger and returned before the injury healed fully. Friendships formed in Press boxes lasted for years, an obvious factor being the time spent there. People know each other far better after three or four days than in the hustle of football matches and the pace is more leisurely. Cricket grounds become associated with the people who will be there and the pubs within range after close of play. It is like working in a time warp, a remnant of Edwardian England. Jeff Brown was one of the journalists who set out with Durham when they were granted first-class status in 1992 and when, after a few years, he left newspapers to join Tyne-Tees Television, he wrote: "Until I covered county cricket, I had no idea that a job could be so much fun." It was a point well made because, when you meet colleagues once or twice a year, there is much ground to be covered, old stories to be revived. Derbyshire offered little excitement in those days: that commodity was reserved for the Baseball Ground but I never for a moment regretted the decision to change careers.

THE PEAK

DERBY County were not overburdened by expectations in 1971-72, although they clearly had the ability to enjoy a successful season and, perhaps, claim the European place denied to them through administrative flaws in 1970. Gradually, the realisation grew that the Rams could do more, that they were in with a chance of becoming Champions for the first time, 88 years since their foundation as an offshoot of the County Cricket Club and 84 years after they were one of the 12 original members of the Football League. The title was clinched when Brian Clough was on holiday with his family in the Scilly Isles and the players were enjoying themselves in Majorca with Peter Taylor. When they completed their programme with a 1-0 victory over Liverpool at the Baseball Ground, two clubs could overtake their 58 points: Leeds United had 57, with a better goal average, and Liverpool 56. Leeds had to meet Arsenal in the FA Cup Final before they could take on Wolverhampton Wanderers at Molineux and, on the same night, Liverpool would face Arsenal at Highbury. The odds were surely against Derby and, for supporters, it was a harrowing night of listening to radio commentaries and praying hard. Amazingly, it came out right for them as Wolves beat Leeds in a ferocious match and Liverpool drew at Highbury. Something pepped up Wolves to deny Leeds the Double, following their 1-0 victory at Wembley, and years later there were accusations of attempted bribery. Revie threatened to sue the newspaper in question but never did and nothing was ever proved. One thing that niggled Clough was the charge that Derby won the

Championship by default but this was such utter drivel that he had no cause to worry. Titles are won over a season and although one night in May was decisive, Derby had more points than anybody else. There has never been an unworthy winner of such a punishing competition.

There are two amazing facts. The Rams used only 16 players and three of them, Tony Bailey, Steve Powell and Jim Walker, made only six starts and four substitute appearances between them. Having said that, Powell's impact as a 16-year-old in the final game against Liverpool was massive and Walker scored an important winner against Crystal Palace at Selhurst Park. The other thing that struck me as remarkable was that, as the tension began to grow, Clough announced he was giving up smoking. He enjoyed cigarettes, as did Taylor, and it was a considerable effort of will. Perhaps he was demonstrating that if he was strong enough to abandon nicotine, players could show the determination to finish at the top of the League. As the Rams also won the Texaco Cup and the Central League, it was a year of unprecedented success. When they held a celebration dinner at the Pennine Hotel, a lady done up to the nines saw the trophies being carried in and said: "How many cups have they won?" That infuriated me because, if she didn't know, she should not have been in there. All the people packed into the street outside had better claims to a ticket but, when this was mentioned in print, there were mutterings from the Council about a sour report. Perhaps this reporter felt a bit sour. A professional comedian, hired for the evening, fell on dead ground but Bob Cass, a North-Eastern journalist who was a long-standing friend of Clough and later helped Jim Smith with his autobiography, had the audience laughing until their ribs hurt. Later, the comedian was seen in earnest conversation with Cass in search of a few tips.

Although Derby were unbeaten in the first 12 League games of the season, they were not entirely convincing. Seven of them were drawn and to see Derby on their better days made it seem that points were allowed to drift away when they were held. They were totally dominant against Newcastle United, a game decided by Alan Hinton's goal, and the North-East Press purred over Colin Todd's display. They had watched Todd develop at Sunderland and he merely confirmed their high opinion of him.

A trip to St James' Park was always enjoyable because so many distinguished players were then covering matches. It was not the place to trumpet dogmatic opinions when the row behind featured Jackie Milburn, Len Shackleton, Albert Stubbins and George Hardwick. Derby lost for the first time at Old Trafford when Frank O'Farrell was presented with his Manager of the Month award. Trying to succeed Sir Matt Busby had already proved too much for Wilf McGuinness and, despite a good start, O'Farrell also struggled to escape the shadow. George Best scored the only goal and, on the day, it was undoubtedly the right result. By then, the Texaco Cup campaign was in progress and Dundee United were seen off 6-2 in the home leg. Terry Hennessey, constantly battling for fitness, flew to the second leg with supporters and, unsurprisingly, creaked at Tannadice Park. When Stoke City were at the Baseball Ground in round two, Steve Powell was included, exactly a month past his 16th birthday. Tommy's son was solidly built and was a Saturday morning attraction when playing for Derby Boys. He padded around, totally in charge of matches, and hardly changed his style when with the professionals. There was a lovely moment in the Stoke game when Hennessey was about to take a throw and Powell trotted across, saying: "Leave it, Terry son." Unusually, Clough and Taylor were slow off the mark in signing Powell. Because Tommy worked in the *Evening Telegraph* accounts department, George Edwards was able to convey to them the intensity of the offers coming in from other clubs, so Clough went to see the headmaster of Bemrose School. Dr Chapman was reluctant to lose Powell, whom he considered to be an Oxbridge candidate, but Clough pointed out that Steve would be able to 'buy bloody Oxford' if he agreed to join the Rams. Powell went on to captain England to victory in the Little World Cup but what promised to be a great international career turned into a very good one at club level. Injuries did not help and Steve did remarkably well to play until 1985. In later years, he went to ground in order to put in a tackle because his knee ligaments hung by a thread. He was a player of immense determination but, sadly, the best things came at the start of his career, when he was hardly old enough to savour them, and much of his time was spent in the club's downward spiral. Alan Lewis, another Youth international, made his debit in the same game but mustered only a handful of appearances before moving to Brighton.

Two penalties from Hinton helped to see off Sheffield United, whose gentlemanly manager John Harris almost forgot himself. "I don't like to complain about referees," he said in the cramped Baseball Ground corridor. As notebooks rose in unison for the second half of the sentence, he offered only one more word, 'but', then sucked his teeth significantly and wandered away. Malcolm Allison was far more forthcoming when Manchester City were beaten 3-1 a fortnight later in a match featuring one of Derby's most memorable goals. Hinton created it and while he held the ball on the left, inviting Tony Book to commit himself, Ron Webster set off on a long run. Webster and the ball arrived simultaneously, a simple header rounding off a moment of perfection. It was his only goal of the season and when the next came in 1974-75, it strengthened hopes of a second Championship success. There were only seven in Webster's 535 appearances but what a terrific career it was. As Clough said: "I don't pay him to score goals. I pay him to keep them out at the other end and he does that quite well." City were at their best when Joe Mercer was manager and Allison the coach but, by this time, Mercer had moved upstairs. "Alan Hinton's cross balls were out of this world," said Allison, who then caused a furore by adding that he was not worried about being five points behind Manchester United because they were a bad side. He turned out to be right but it was an essentially light-hearted session in which Clough likened goalkeeper Joe Corrigan to 'a bad journalist without a pencil'. Having unpicked City by stealth, Hinton sorted out Everton by ferocious shooting but there was a major setback when Derby were well beaten by Leeds at Elland Road two days after Christmas. Leeds were a class ahead and it was time for Clough to have public doubts about the determination and moral fibre of his players. The points was made and accepted, Derby losing only three of their remaining 19 League games, but that was an outstanding Leeds team. If Gary Sprake dropped an occasional spectacular clanger, he was good enough to play more than 500 times in goal. Paul Reaney, Paul Madeley, Jack Charlton, Norman Hunter and Terry Cooper were available in defence: Billy Bremner and John Giles were the fulcrum in midfield, with Peter Lorimer, who scored 238 goals for the club, and Eddie Gray wide: Mick Jones and Allan Clarke were the strikers. There is no obvious weakness in that team but, although Revie was a fine manager, the paternal intensity of his methods produced too many frustrated near-misses. Those players needed somebody to tell them to go out and enjoy themselves.

Derby were handily placed when the FA Cup began and also faced a Texaco Cup Final against Airdrieonians. Tony Parry, just signed from Hartlepool, found himself in a different world, flying to make his debut, although a quasi-international competition more closely resembled the old Third Division North as the teams pitched in for a hectic 0-0. As Hennessey revelled in the scrap, an Aidrie fan bawled at him: "That number six. Just gi' us his body." In the fourth round of the FA Cup, Derby drew neighbours Notts County, not long promoted from the Third Division as Jimmy Sirrel maintained the remarkable run of success he began with Brentford. In terms of points-per-game, nobody could beat him. I asked Clough and Taylor, before going to Meadow Lane for an interview, how such an ordinary player could turn into a winning manager. "You ask him," said Clough. "He likes people to be direct." The sight of Taylor chuckling to himself suggested a more tactful phrasing of the question but Sirrel managed to throw me by describing himself as one of the finest players ever to come out of Scotland. That did not quite tally with a career that, after a few games for Celtic, took in Bradford, Brighton and Aldershot. Notts were seen off 6-0 and Derby were paired with Arsenal, the Double winners of 1970-71. There were two draws and the second, at Highbury, attracted a crowd of 63,077 despite a midweek afternoon kick-off because of a power crisis. In the third meeting, on neutral ground at Filbert Street, an ill-judged back pass by John McGovern let in Ray Kennedy for the only goal. I was among many who thought a Cup exit no bad thing, because Derby's squad was so small, but Clough was furious. "He never let me forget it," said McGovern years later. "He was still lobbing that in when we were together with Forest." Clough and Taylor attempted to boost their resources at the beginning of March when it became clear that Nottingham Forest, heading for relegation, would sell Ian Storey-

Moore. It was unlikely to be a straightforward transaction because, after selling Hennessey to Derby, Forest dug their heels in and steered Henry Newton towards Everton. Something similar soon happened with Storey-Moore, as Manchester United were also prepared to pay £200,000. Even so, Derby had permission to talk to Storey-Moore, who was keen to join them, thought the decision was left with him and signed the transfer forms. Only a signature from Forest was needed to complete the transaction but they refused to give it and the Rams took a tremendous gamble. Storey-Moore joined the players at the Midland Hotel the night before the home game against Wolverhampton Wanderers but Forest refused to budge. "It was decided that we should take Ian on the pitch," said Stuart Webb, then secretary, "so Peter and I did that. It was a big risk but Brian and Peter felt Forest were in such disarray that it would force them to back down. We took another club's player and virtually held him hostage at the Midland over the weekend." Storey-Moore, despite being introduced to the crowd as a new signing, never joined Derby and, sadly, his United career was cut short by injury. The Football League fined Derby £5,000 for their actions and, when later back with Forest as chief scout, Storey-Moore said: "Derby had some wonderful players, I signed the form and would love to have joined them. The whole thing was bizarre. I still wonder where I would have played. Alan Hinton was doing extremely well on the left, they had John O'Hare and Kevin Hector up front. From what I know of Clough and Taylor, I might well have been on the bench."

Hinton, with a penalty, and McFarland earned the points off Wolves that day and, before the Cup exit, Derby beat Tottenham Hotspur at White Hart Lane. A 0-0 draw was on the cards until a late error by Pat Jennings gave the Rams a penalty, another expertly put away by Hinton. It kept them in step with Manchester City and Leeds in early March, when it began to dawn on the players that the title was a distinct possibility. There was another important 1-0 in London before the month was out, when Jim Walker's goal beat Crystal Palace. It was scant reward for Derby's uninhibited attacking, especially in the first half, and they were also forced to show they could defend as Palace hung in. Walker, signed from Northwich Victoria in 1968, was a squad player by the time the Championship came round. His attraction for Clough and Taylor was an ability to hold the ball, even if his runs often took him across rather than up the field. He was proud of that goal and when a title race is as close as this one, many can claim decisive interventions. Walker trained as a physiotherapist and has been with Aston Villa for 16 years. He lends a sympathetic ear to Villa players and the bargain is that they listen to his stories about Dave Mackay in the Baseball Ground days.

Victory at Selhurst Park set up the Easter games, with the big clash first. On the Saturday, Derby beat Leeds with as complete a performance as they produced all season. Only memories of Leeds' previous dominance kept the Baseball Ground crowd on edge, because they were watching the Rams in control. McGovern shackled Giles and Kevin Hector played wider than usual, keeping Cooper fully occupied so that he was prohibited from making the forward runs so essential to his side. For once, Leeds were the team pulled around and made to defend desperately. John O'Hare was involved in both goals. He scored the first in the 16th minute after John Robson hurried Bremner into a mistake and Alan Durban clipped in a perfect cross. The second, after 69 minutes, was an own goal by Hunter, rough justice after he did so much too keep Leeds afloat. Hector's darting run ended with a diagonal pass to O'Hare, whose shot hit Sprake, rattled against Hunter's shins and rolled into the net. No blame could be attached to Big Norman, who was desperately trying to recover in an overstretched defence. There was a long night in the Press room, where the affable John Lloyd was in charge of a generous bar, and talk, for as long as it remained coherent, was about the Championship. The match, with its obvious importance, took a lot out of Derby and they were unable to reproduce those standards when, two days later, they lost at home to Newcastle. There was one holiday game left, at West Bromwich on the Wednesday. A dry, bare pitch and a swirling wind meant it was not much of a spectacle but a 0-0 kept Derby on top, a point clear with four games left, although the pursuers all had five to go. It was a good time to reel off two comprehensive victories, 4-0 over Sheffield United at Bramall Lane and 3-0 against Huddersfield Town at home, but there was still a twist to come. Manchester City, once firm favourites for the title, lost their way in April after Malcolm Allison signed Rodney Marsh from Queen's Park Rangers and therefore had to integrate a highly individual talent into a team that was working very well without it. Later, Allison was to lament that he was surprised by Marsh's lack of fitness but the manager could not resist an urge to tinker. Even among Sky Television's comprehensive collection of experts who failed as managers, Marsh stands out because he never tried to do the job. That does not stop him telling others how to do it, despite a history as the kind of player to turn his boss prematurely grey. One of Harry Storer's truisms was: "There's nothing worse than a goalscorer who's not scoring goals." The reasoning, that expectation is not matched by reality, could easily be extended to the lavishly gifted individual who is unreliable. There was no doubt that Marsh could play when the wind was in his sails, as it was in the 2-0 victory against Derby that day. He swayed away from McFarland and Robson to hit the first goal wide of Boulton and was brought down by Hennessey to give Francis Lee a chance from the penalty spot. City went to the top but it was their last game and they could not win the title because Derby or Liverpool would overtake them after their May Day meeting at the Baseball Ground.

Webster's injury at Maine Road created a vacancy at right-back and Clough, bold as ever, handed the job to Steve Powell. It was a fine, tense match between two excellent teams and, over the years, three memories persist. One is of Powell flicking the ball over Emlyn Hughes and, as he gathered it, looking for the next pass. Through 90 minutes, Powell performed superbly, so well that his age ceased to be a consideration. McGovern scored the only goal after 62 minutes, only his third of the season. Gemmill accepted a throw and went across the penalty area in search of the vital opening. He had to turn back on himself before finding Durban, whose dummy offered McGovern the chance to fire a shot wide of Ray Clemence. It was a tremendous goal and McGovern raced away with his ungainly, stiff-backed run, one arm in the air to celebrate. Even when he was lifting European Cup as captain of Nottingham Forest, there was always something coltish about McGovern: he remained Young John until the day he retired, a permanent student playing at the highest level of club football. The final act belong to Durban, who was in a covering position to clear when Boulton stretched to push out John McLaughlin's effort. We were used to Durban being cerebral in midfield and making late glides into the opposition penalty area but this was not his usual territory. It was Liverpool's last throw and, at the end, the crowd knew they were assured of European football and had a chance of winning the Championship. They were also aware that Clough and Taylor were to stay at the Baseball Ground after rejecting an offer, not the first, from Coventry City's ambitious chairman Derrick Robins. Less notice was taken of a decision by the executors of Ossie Jackson, a former chairman, to sell two-thirds of his shares to Jack Kirkland. Longson was unhappy: "I thought the executors would let the board know before taking important action like this," he said. The purchase, along with others, made Kirkland the second biggest shareholder and 18 months later, his malevolent influence was instrumental in sparking a major crisis. In May, 1972, supporters did not have boardroom politics on their mind because they saw a triumphant conclusion to a memorable season and had a week to consider if their team could stay at the top. There was a sense of wonderment when it fell into place: was this really happening to us? It was not simply European football coming to Derby but the European Cup which was strictly limited, unlike the contemporary Champions' League, to League Champions. That precious ticket was earned by a small band of talented players, who blended perfectly and showed hardly a weakness. Clough gave them stick after the Christmas defeat at Leeds, when he wrote in *The Ram*, a newspaper that superseded the conventional programme: "I think they believe they can rely on their skills to keep them playing until they're 90. If they go on like this, they won't be playing for me for another nine months. I bought them and put them together, with the prime consideration of their skills in mind. Yet every player must face it that in certain situations and against some opposition, they must be prepared for a physical challenge. We shall never win the League Championship unless all our players are prepared to show this basic quality, the same as all the players with the other title contenders." They took notice – it's called management – and the battered old trophy belonged to Derby for the first time.

Colin Boulton and Kevin Hector played in every match, John Robson missed only one, Colin Todd, Archie Gemmill and John O'Hare each clocked up 40. There was consistency at all levels, in playing performances, selection and management thinking. The act of writing about the season 31 years later serves to remind me just how good a team that was, what fun it was to watch and how easy were the professional dealings with management and players. There was no need then for a Press Office, while the staffing for training and administration would now be regarded as subsistence level. Jimmy Gordon and Gordon Guthrie looked after the fitness while finding time to take in other associated activities, such as the kit. Jimmy, unused to dealing with the media in his playing days, could be dour but once revealed a wicked sense of humour by suggesting I helped myself to a cup of tea in the dressing-room after training. Clough was unimpressed by my presence, as in 'Get your tea and f*** off out of here,' and I almost dropped the giant pot in my eagerness to comply. As Jimmy knew perfectly well, I had no business in there but he finished with an impressive array of medals after rejoining Clough at the City Ground. One of the best sights was to see him lead out Forest at Wembley for their third consecutive League Cup Final, probably with that nervous little cough of his on the way. There were times, when Clough and Taylor blasted players, that Jimmy acted as the favourite uncle to pick them up ahead of the next challenge. Derby had no need of a sports psychologist because Clough did that. "We would win on a Saturday and he told us to go out and enjoy ourselves," McFarland recalled, "but he always planted a seed as well. He would tell us not to forget we had another game the following Wednesday and it worked because we went home sooner than we really wanted." The title was decided while everybody was away but they opened the Baseball Ground on a Sunday morning to parade the trophies and about 15,000 came to watch. It was all gradually sinking in that, after years of being unambitious mediocrities, Derby were at the top of the tree. The trouble with the club is that they are at their worst when handling success but there was another big adventure to come before it all went wrong.

Through a few studiedly casual references during summer, my European Cup plans were laid. The hope was that I could alternate with George Edwards for the away games and even that, I felt, was pushing my luck. When it turned out that I went on all the trips, there was no point in questioning the decision or asking for reasons. It was a matter staying quiet and thanking my lucky stars. There was no resemblance to the contemporary, television driven, Champions' League, just two rounds before Christmas and two more before the Final when hostilities resumed in the New Year. When the European Cup was first played in 1955, Derby were in the Third Division North and nobody even thought of suggesting that they would one day compete with the finest teams on the Continent: anyway, the game against Gateshead was coming up. The competition gained status from the first of several great Real Madrid teams, winners for five consecutive years. It was rare then for club teams to be multinational but Real followed a policy of trying to engage the best players in the world, fine provided they could link with Alfredo Di Stefano. He was the king of the Bernabeu Stadium and a forward of supreme talent, backed by boundless stamina which made him active all round the field. After the crushing of the Hungarian Revolution, Ferenc Puskas found a way to earn Di Stefano's respect by offering him a tap-in instead of completing the job himself: Didi, signed after Brazil's World Cup triumph in Sweden, was not so lucky. When Matt Busby began his quest to bring the European Cup to Manchester, he described Real as the best team he had ever seen. Busby endured the nightmare of the Munich disaster in 1958 before reaching his goal 10 years later with victory over Benfica at Wembley. Celtic, under Jock Stein and fielding a team all born within 30 miles of Glasgow, beat him to it by 12 months. In 1972-73, English hopes rested on Derby County, demanding a huge leap of the imagination for those who went to the Baseball Ground to see them take on Accrington Stanley, Bradford (Park Avenue), Southport and the rest only 16 years earlier. Derby folk can be reticent and the first game in Europe, against Zeljeznicar Sarajevo, attracted only 27,350. It was a dangerous tie because Yugoslavian teams, before we had to sort out who were Bosnians, Serbs or Croats, had a reputation for mixing skill on the ball with ferocity when they did not have it. It was clear from the first leg that Zeljeznicar did not defend well and their goalkeeper was unhappy when Hinton chipped or drove in a series of perfect centres. Derby's 2-0 lead was comforting, if not decisive, and they travelled optimistically to the town where the assassination of Archduke Franz Ferdinand sparked World War One. The two smells of Eastern Europe hit them at the airport, those of strong tobacco and that kind of raw petrol that made cars pink like an old sewing machine, as I knew from an earlier holiday which took in Budapest. Slivovitz, a ferocious plum brandy, was a new taste to explore but it was an error to try it in company with such experienced professionals as Geoffrey Green, the wonderful football correspondent of *The Times*, and Alan Williams, the *Daily Express* man in the Midlands. It was a meeting of cultures, mosques as well as churches, markets in which bartering was expected, taxi drivers steering battered Mercedes through crowded streets at alarming speeds. Zeljeznicar tried to make life difficult: there were no balls for training until Clough opened a cupboard and they tumbled out: goalmouths were returfed before the game in an attempt to embarrass defenders. Derby coped with everything and effectively settled the tie in the first 15 minutes with goals from Hinton and O'Hare. They needed their discipline because Zeljeznicar's approach was nasty enough to make it surprising that they finished with as many as 10 men. As the flight back was not until Thursday, journalists took the players to the Ham-Am nightclub but beat a strategic retreat when Kevin Hector, unimpressed by the belly-dancer, put his foot through a drum. We did remember to take the King with us but there was a different approach from the Press in the early 70s, more on parade and off parade, so Hector's indiscretion went unreported: now the tabloids would be blowing up their headlines. Victory earned the Rams a glamorous tie with Benfica, winners twice, Finalists on another three occasions, the team of Eusebio. Fleet Street chortled that Derby would be put in their place, Clough and Taylor went to Portugal to view the oppo-sition. When they returned Clough was, for once, strictly off the record. "I daren't tell you how bad they are," he said, "and I certainly can't let on to them," his thumb waved in the direction of the dressing-room. Benfica had an English coach, Jimmy Hagan, who set out at Derby in the 1930s before constructing a wonderful career with Sheffield United. He won many Wartime caps but one full international was a derisory reward for one of the best inside-forwards of his time. He and Benfica expected to win but they were blasted out of sight on a sodden Baseball Ground. Sir Stanley Rous, then president of FIFA, commented on the conditions and Taylor told him there had been a local storm: too right, because it was caused by the Derby Fire Brigade, who gave the pitch a thorough soaking. McFarland headed Derby in front, Hector instinctively volleyed in the second, McGovern scored a third. It was over by half-time and Malcolm Allison, big cigar in hand, uttered only one word as he came down from the directors' box at the interval: "Unbelievable." A day earlier, Hector could hardly walk down the Baseball Ground corridor. He had a spinal injection and was brilliant: *L'Equipe* wrote of: "Kevin Hector, aux pieds agile, qui poseret un probleme permanent aux defendeurs lisbonais." That was one of the nights, along with the League Cup victory over Chelsea and the defeat of Real Madrid, that supporters remembered when they talked of the unique atmosphere of the Baseball Ground. The emotion reached out and clawed at people but, because it was such an up and down club, there were also games played out there in an air of mutual suspicion between participants and observers. Benfica still fancied themselves and there was a timely warning from Ronnie Allen, the former West Bromwich and England centre-forward who managed rivals Sporting Lisbon. "Benfica are one of the greatest teams I have ever seen when they are going forward," said Allen. "Like all great sides, they score goals in bunches." This time, they were staunched by Colin Boulton and Terry Hennessey. Three times in the first half-hour, Eusebio was in and three times, the goalkeeper won the battle. Hennessey was in his best spell at Derby, before injury again overtook him, and his bald head was like a lighthouse sending out safety signals. It was a great defensive display by the whole team and Clough said: "Even if we'd been issued with those Belgian sub-machine guns they give to NATO, we couldn't have stopped them. There just seemed to be waves of red shirts." Perhaps Benfica were better than Clough estimated but, by silencing 75,000 in the Estadio da Luz, Derby earned respectful glances around Europe.

The next round, in March, took Derby into less known territory to face the Czechoslovakian champions Spartak Trnava. They were similar to the Rams in many way, a provincial club who hit the top, but they had a good

Nine of the team which Derby County fielded in the first match I saw, in January 1946. This side is pictured eight weeks later, at Coventry before a Football League South game in which Vic Woodley, signed to cover a goalkeeping emergency, made his Rams debut. Back row (left to right): Dave Willis (trainer), Jimmy Bullions, Jack Parr, Vic Woodley, Angus Morrison, Chick Musson, Dally Duncan. Front row: Reg Harrison, Raich Carter, Leon Leuty, Jack Nicholas, Peter Doherty, John Shearer. The Rams had signed Carter and Doherty three months earlier, just in time to be eligible for that season's FA Cup. Shearer was one of those players who flitted in and out of Derby's story during wartime. It was his only appearance for them; he later played a handful of League games for Bradford City and Grimsby Town.

Victory parade. The men immortalised in Derby County's history as the only Rams team to win the FA Cup are pictured on their way through Derby with the trophy, carried by skipper Jack Nicholas. The players were driven into town on board an Offiler's beer dray before appearing on the balcony of the police station in Full Street. The Council House was not yet completed after war held up building work.

The Rams team that reached the 1948 FA Cup semi-final, where they beaten by Manchester United at Hillsborough. Back row (left to right): Stuart McMillan (manager), Tim Ward, Bert Mozley, Leon Leuty, Jock Wallace, Jack Howe, Chick Musson, Jack Poole (trainer). Front row: Reg Harrison, Raich Carter, Jack Stamps, Billy Steel, Angus Morrison. Scotland international Steel, a British record signing, was an unpopular figure in the dressing-room.

Despite the presence of Walter Winterbottom, England manager and FA Director of Coaching, this schools course in 1953 did not lead to great things. I am near the back on the left, hoping others did not realise I was out of my class. Two future Derby County players, Peter Newbery and John Bowers, are near the front right.

St Catherine's Society, Oxford, English group of 1957, trying to pretend they were Victorians. Tom Phillips (back left) became a distinguished painter, and Reg Hill (centre, back) earned fame for his Dalziel and Pascoe novels. I am front right.

National Service meant that I missed most of Derby County's time in the Third Division North from 1955 to 1957. One result we awaited eagerly in Sennelager, West Germany, was on Easter Monday 1957 when the Rams beat Chesterfield 7-1 at the Baseball Ground. A crowd of almost 30,000 saw Derby all but clinch promotion back to the Second Division. Here Ray Straw scores one of his hat-trick goals against the Rams' Derbyshire neighbours.

Manager Tim Ward signs Newcastle United winger Gordon Hughes for £10,000 in August 1963. Ward brought some excellent players to Derby including Alan Durban, Eddie Thomas and Colin Boulton, the goalkeeper who was ever-present in two League Championships under Brian Clough and then Dave Mackay. Ward's greatest signing, though, was Kevin Hector from Bradford. When he resigned in May 1967, Ward complained that he was unable to use so much as a twopenny stamp without asking the board. A former Rams player and England international, he loved the club and later ran the ex-Rams team – he was still playing into his 60s – and was the instigator of the Former Players' Association, of which he was chairman until his death.

The start of something big. Rams chairman Sam Longson poses proudly with Brian Clough and Peter Taylor outside the Baseball Ground in May 1967. Even Longson could not have imagined just how Derby County would be transformed over the next five years. Nor could anyone have foreseen the bitter end to his relationship with the most successful manager in the club's history.

Clough and new chairman Sydney Bradley, together with Derby players, look on as Dave Mackay is presented with the Second Division championship trophy by Football League chairman Len Shipman of Leicester City.

In the summer of 1969 the Ley Stand rose up over the Popular Side, the first major development at the Baseball Ground since before the Second World War. So fierce was interest in the Rams that supporters were prepared to buy two-year season tickets to ensure a place in the new stand. This picture shows Alan Durban and Kevin Hector (10) in action during the 1-0 win over Burnley in September 1970

On a Sunday morning in May 1972, the Baseball Ground was opened to tens of thousands of Derby County supporters who came to see Brian Clough's team parade the League Championship trophy, won by the club for the first time in its history. The team had flown in from Majorca where they had been on holiday when both Liverpool and Leeds failed at their final hurdles. Also on show are the Texaco and Central League trophies.

Derby County in a European Cup semi-final? Six years earlier the Rams had been playing the likes of Northampton, Hull and Bury in the Second Division, but in April 1973 they stepped out at the Stadio Communale in Turin to take on the Italian champions, Juventus. Amidst an allegation of attempted bribery of referees, Derby eventually lost the semi-final tie but the occasion was a measure of just how far the club had come. Here Kevin Hector is pictured with Roberto Bettega (left) and Sandro Salvadore.

In October 1973, the unthinkable happened. Brian Clough and Peter Taylor left Derby County after a very public falling-out with Sam Longson. There followed public meetings, protest marches around the town and even a strike threat by the Rams players. The pair, though, were on their way out of Derby, and former favourite Dave Mackay stepped into a very difficult situation.

Before the final game of the 1974-75 season, against Carlisle United when the Rams were to be crowned champions again and later the infamous Baseball Ground pitch dug up, former Derby players linked arms to sign *Auld Lang Syne*. It was a glittering occasion and, sadly, one never to be repeated. Every generation from the end of the First World War to the present day was represented.

side. There was a foot-and-mouth scare, so everybody had to walk over pads of disinfectant at the border before a featureless trip up the Danube valley to the small Slovakian town. By then, there was an important change in Derby's team as David Nish became eligible for Europe. Clough was a long-term admirer of Leicester City's full-back and finally gatecrashed a meeting of their board to announce he had come to sign him. It cost Derby £225,000, their first British record since the days of Billy Steel and Johnny Morris, but they were buying pedigree. He joined them in August, 1972, and initially struggled to find his feet. Nish was first with the team at Norwich and when lunchtime television showed a brilliant break for Leicester, with a shot just over the bar, Archie Gemmill piped up: "Christ, what a chance that was." After one match, Nish went back to the Midland Hotel with the other players and was so depressed about his form that he piled into the Scotches, explaining: "I've tried everything else." Quality prevailed before long and John Robson, who did a tremendous job, was sold to Aston Villa in December, 1972. It was a good move for Robson, with the £90,000 fee then the highest Derby had received. There was a promotion in 1975, along with League Cup successes then and two years later, but his career was curtailed in 1978 by multiple sclerosis. Since the Former Players' Association was formed, Robson has unfailingly attended the dinners, on sticks but remarkably cheerful. Spartak won the first leg 1-0, leaving Derby dented but still confident of progress, although they acknowledged that the Czechs were the most skilful team they had met so far. Two goals from Kevin Hector saw them through but only after a hard match. Derby defended splendidly, by no means a feature of their League season, and for all the anxiety, Colin Boulton did not have a direct shot to save.

Between the two legs of the Spartak Trnava game, Derby went out of the FA Cup to their great rivals Leeds United but I missed the classic replay victory over Tottenham Hotspur in February. Over 32 years, I was absent from very few games but had booked a holiday in Scotland and therefore failed to see the hat-trick that announced Roger Davies as a future star. Davies cost £12,000, then a record for a non-League player, when Derby signed him from Worcester City and he had a considerable impact as Derby won the Central League in 1971-72, as well as making a League debut while on loan to Preston North End. For a tall man, he had great ball control and gradually began to push John O'Hare for a place in attack. He earned a Championship medal in 1974-75 before Dave Mackay sold him to Club Brugge, who won the Belgian League and Cup double with him in the side. Davies also played in the United States, for Tulsa Roughnecks, Seattle Sounders and Fort Lauderdale Strikers, fitting in a second spell at Derby under Colin Addison. His value was multiplied by ten in his first five years at Derby, again emphasising Peter Taylor's ability to spot players in the unlikeliest settings. Victory over Spartak elevated Derby to the European summit, with a semi-final against Juventus, and they took John Charles with them for the first leg in Turin. It was almost 16 years since the Welsh international swapped Leeds for Juventus and became the most successful British export to Italy, with three Championship medals. The affection for him was moving: Charles stopped the traffic and disrupted big department stores because everybody wanted to see him and applaud this charming man with the deep Welsh voice. If that was a shrewd public relations stroke, little else went right for Derby, starting with a venomous row between Clough and Taylor. They were due to attend a formal dinner for the Press but, having dressed for the occasion, Taylor found Clough in his training gear, playing cards with the team and refusing to budge. Taylor was livid then and alarmed next day at the Stadio Comunale when he was arrested by Italian police. He spotted Helmut Haller, a German World Cup Finalist in 1966 and then a Juventus player, in conversation with the German referee, Gerhardt Schulenburg, both before the game and, more suspiciously, at half-time. By the interval, Archie Gemmill and Roy McFarland had been booked for trivial offences, ruling both out of the second leg. It had every appearance of a put-up job, although later revelations concentrated on attempts to bribe the Portuguese referee, Lobo, before the game at Derby. Following the 3-1 defeat, Clough raged at 'cheating bastards' but there was no masking the expertise with which Jose Altafini put away two chances. O'Hare played magnificently but the one shred of hope was Hector's goal, the first by an English club in a European Cup tie in Italy. Because of that, a 2-0 victory at the Baseball Ground would put Derby through to the Final in Belgrade but it was a situation made for the defensively orientated Italian football of the 1970s. A goal would have tightened the situation and there was a chance when Spinosi tripped Hector. Hinton, back after a month out through injury, put the penalty well wide and, six minutes later, Davies was sent off for butting Morini, the culmination of a running battle throughout the match. Derby faced the last 27 minutes with 10 men, making an already difficult task impossible. When Clough criticised Hinton for missing the penalty, it struck me as manifestly unfair in view of the winger's contribution towards turning Derby from a Second Division club to Champions and European Cup semi-finalists. Having written in that vein, I wondered if the next meeting with the manager would be prickly. Instead, it was warm: "I'm glad you wrote that," he said. "I'd have thought less of you if you hadn't." It was a gift for the unexpected that kept players alert although, it should be noted, there was no suggestion that he had been wrong. Several years later, I covered Nottingham Forest's European Cup tie in Sofia for *The Times* and telephone problems for all the journalists meant the team flight was held up. We expected him to be furious but he was concerned only with our difficulties. When George Edwards retired as editor of the *South Wales Evening Post* in Swansea, he recalled the times he was asked if there were any particular memories from his association with Clough and Taylor. In his speech, he said that dealing with them provided one long anecdote and, in 1973, we expected that to continue. Derby were wiser for the experience of playing Juventus, who lost the Final when Ajax of Amsterdam completed a hat-trick of victories to increase Clough's frustration. An average League season left them seventh and out of Europe, because Leeds were beaten by Sunderland in the FA Cup Final, but surely they would be back under this management. Depression would have swamped Derby had we realised how close was the end for Clough and Taylor as, not for the first of last time, the boardroom succumbed to stubborn incompetence.

There was already a change at the *Derby Telegraph*, when Edwards stepped up to become assistant-editor. His deputy, Ian James, should have become sports editor but did not want the job, so I was approached.

Having made it clear that there was no intention of giving up football and cricket coverage, I agreed to give it a try and stayed in the post until 1994 when a new editor, Mike Lowe, decided he wanted sport run from within the office. That was a perfectly sound decision and, looking back, it is clear I owed a great deal to various deputies such as Jeff Humphreys, Steve Gill, Simon Farrington, Mark Tattersall and Steve Nicholson. It was selfish to sit on three plum positions but, having entered journalism to be involved with Derby County and Derbyshire, there was no inclination to become an office worker. Not that Derbyshire were thrilling me. In 1972, they were bottom of the Championship for the second year in succession and changed captaincy, with Brian Bolus taking over from Ian Buxton for the following season. Bolus, originally with Yorkshire, enjoyed good times at Nottinghamshire and played in seven Tests for England. At his best, he was an opening batsman capable of dominating an attack but, if out of touch, was one of the worst good players it is possible to imagine. He was always known for the way he used his front pad, blocking balls to release a cloud of whitening, and it was rumoured that he wore out five pairs of pads to every bat. As captain, he was talkative, approachable but prone to changes of theory. Famously, he sent Alan Ward from the field in the game against Yorkshire at Queen's Park in June, 1973. Ward, who had been shelled by John Hampshire, refused to return for a second spell so Bolus, having already left the field to consult the secretary, Major Douglas Carr, waved him off. It was only the third instance in first-class cricket of a player being disciplined in this way by his captain and, obviously, the Press box was agog. The Major produced one of the classic quotes: "I can confirm that Alan Ward has left the field," he said, stating what occasioned the original question to him. Beyond that, he would not be drawn but Ward later apologised for his behaviour and announced his retirement. As it turned out, he stayed with Derbyshire until 1976 and made another Test appearance, against West Indies that year. He was and remains a delightful man, with a talent to bowl fast that was unsupported by the necessary destructive urge. At least Derbyshire moved off the bottom under Bolus but it was by only one place, a point ahead of Nottinghamshire. Their policy did raise doubts. In a spurt of ambition, they tried to sign Dennis Lillee, the great Australian fast bowler, for 1973. When Lillee's back injury made this impossible, they moved instead for the Indian off-spinner Srinivasaraghavan Venkataraghavan, although they had two other off-spinners, Bob Swindell and the emerging Geoff Miller on the staff. Venkat, in the tradition of thoroughly civilised Indian players, gave Derbyshire three good years but it did make one wonder where Derbyshire's priorities lay. He had a unique career because, having played for, captained and managed India, he then became a Test umpire, totally calm in his slightly lugubrious way. He also paid me one of the greatest compliments of my life when he was leading an Indian touring team and I invited him for a meal in Nottingham. He started to recommend dishes as the staff, agitated by the appearance of a star, buzzed around, then said: "But I cannot tell you anything about Indian food." He could, of course, but that was friend for life territory.

MACKAY TO THE
RESCUE

THERE were a few indications that all was not well at the Baseball Ground. Brian Clough, for example, suddenly pulled out of the 1972 pre-season trip because the board would not allow him to take members of his family. His television appearances and newspaper articles were more divisive because Sam Longson collected the backwash from other clubs. Clough attracted the media because he was fluent and opinionated: there would be nothing bland for cameras or notebooks and ITV made it their business to lure him across from the BBC. At a time when Longson felt he should be basking in credit as chairman during the most successful era in Derby County's history, he was being given stick by his peers. Longson always fancied a place on the League Management Committee and saw his chances fade with questions like: "Who's running Derby, you or that bloody man Clough?" Longson once stuck his neck out for Clough, forcing the resignation of three directors, but began to fear his power was being eroded. Jack Kirkland, whose eager buying of shares earlier worried the chairman, had been overheard to say that he planned to bury Clough. Kirkland, a successful building contractor, made boardroom opposition more formidable although, 30 years on, it remains hard to fathom his motives. He was the man who beckoned Peter Taylor across a crowded boardroom after Derby beat Manchester United at Old Trafford and demanded a meeting to explore his job specification. It was intended to be provocative and Taylor bit because he thought, reasonably enough, that the Championship and a European Cup semi-final gave a fair return from the management team. Clough and Taylor underestimated the danger, thinking that they could sweep aside opposition on a popular mandate. Had it been left to supporters, there was only one possible answer but shares dictated the power and the Bass Breweries holding, always pitched behind the directors, gave them the majority. It came to a head when, after the League warned Derby that they were responsible for their manager's public opinions, Clough received a letter ordering him to clear every television appearance and newspaper article with the board. The practical difficulties of that were never considered, so furious was Clough about a restriction on free speech. Derby beat Manchester United on October 13, 1973. Two days later, I went to the Baseball Ground to prepare, I thought, a preview of England's last chance World Cup qualifying match against Poland. About 10 hours later, I emerged, having typed out resignation letters for Clough and Taylor as the office staff had long gone. My advice – don't resign, leave the next move to them – was ignored and Jeff Farmer's exclusive, for which the *Daily Mail* paid, was about to make the Baseball Ground the centre of the universe.

The board's priority was to appoint a new manager because, for as long as there was a vacuum, Clough and Taylor were there to fill it. Jimmy Gordon was in temporary charge for the next game, at home to Leicester City and Clough appeared briefly in the main stand before the start. As the cheers rang out, Longson also stood to acknowledge them and his belief that they were for him made many question his sanity or sobriety. Clough's appearance was fleeting because he was on his way to London to appear on Michael Parkinson's television programme. Bill Holmes, a former amateur international, had a briefer part, arrested when he walked on the pitch to protest at the board's decision: as few were aware of his identity, it was a futile exercise. Bobby Robson was Derby's first target but, impressed though he was by the playing staff, he looked at the way the club was run and decided he would be better off staying with the Cobbolds at Ipswich. Much time was spent waiting on the pavement outside the Baseball Ground but it was sometimes hard to know where to be at a given time. There were farewell parties given by Clough and Taylor at the Midland and Newton Park Hotels, a Protest Movement holding meetings that had the fervour of a religious revival, marches to the ground. The board's saviour was near at hand because, after a brief spell in charge of Swindon Town, Dave Mackay succeeded Matt Gillies as manager of Nottingham Forest. Mackay's feats as a player were fresh in the memory of Derby fans and the board felt he was the man to push the threat of Clough into the background. When some directors went to the City Ground to tie up a deal after a night match, Jack Kirkland and Stuart Webb, the secretary, were locked in the boardroom as players, angered by the refusal to speak to them, patrolled the corridors. Roy McFarland even rang Mackay and asked him not to take the job, in the belief that Clough and Taylor would be reinstated. Having played at the top, Mackay wanted to manage at the same level and was not a man to shy away from difficulties but if the board felt an appointment would draw a line under the Clough affair, disappointment was close. At this stage, Clough was unduly manipulative and players, obviously influenced by the success he brought them, went along with it. There was even a threat by the players that they would withdraw their labour before the game against Leeds United in November as a protest against the current management and a plea to have the former regime reinstated. Fortunately for them, this came to nothing and they were in on the Thursday to apologise to Mackay and his assistant, Des Anderson. "Everybody's entitled to make mistakes and we've made ours in the last two days," said Alan Hinton. By then, Clough and Taylor were in charge of Brighton and Hove Albion, so the reality was that, rightly or wrongly, their days at Derby were over. Taylor found that easier to accept than Clough and wanted to tackle the job at the Goldstone Ground. He stayed when Clough moved to Leeds United for an ill-fated 44 days but there were greater conquests when they were reunited with Nottingham Forest.

That Derby were infinitely luckier than they deserved to be is entirely due to Mackay's personality and, indeed, courage. His first match in charge, against West Ham United at Upton Park ended in a 0-0 draw but his cause was hardly helped by Longson's idiotic remark: "I could manage this lot." Apart from a failure to see the point of having a manager, Longson should have realised Mackay needed every bit of support. Early results did not help him and Anderson. Derby were knocked out of the League Cup in a second replay at Sunderland, with players irritated that the managers tossed for home advantage rather than settling for a neutral venue, and went for six League games without a victory after the upheaval. The spell was broken when they beat Newcastle United 2-0 at St James' Park. Clough's final signing was Henry Newton, who came the long way round. Derby originally wanted to take him from Nottingham Forest, who refused to deal and instead sold him to Everton. He wondered what he had let himself in for but it came out well for him eventually, as it did for Mackay's first capture. While at Swindon, Rod Thomas established himself as a Welsh international defender and played under Mackay, who both liked him as a player and, in all probability, wanted a friendly face in the dressing-room. Thomas, a convivial man, had a long wait before he could displace Ron Webster, illustrating Mackay's essential fairness. Webster was performing well and the shirt was his for as long as he continued, unless injury took a hand. The problems and protests were not really aimed at Mackay, because it was impossible to dislike him. He was not Brian Clough, that was the kernel of the matter: players and a huge majority of supporters wanted Clough back at the Baseball Ground. Mackay stepped round the land mines with skill and composure, recognising the value of patience in a unique situation. Clough later came to regret that he did not support Mackay instead of pursuing his own campaign. "David Mackay did a wonderful job at Derby," he said, "and I did not help him as I should have done." Nor did the local media and I, for one, remained convinced that Clough should never have gone. There was also a reluctance to give any credit to those directors or to a constant irritant, *The Ram*. For several years, the club replaced the traditional programme with a newspaper format that made Pravda look like the independent voice of the Soviet Republic. It was a forerunner of a later development when clubs formed Press offices, usually expanding empires dedicated to putting a favourable spin on such news as they chose to release and limiting access to managers or players.

Mackay made his first major signing in February, 1974, when Derby paid Aston Villa £200,000 for Bruce Rioch to add goals from midfield. At the age of 26, Rioch was approaching his peak and later became captain of Scotland, having an international qualification through his father, a Regimental Sergeant Major imposing enough to take my mind back to Eaton Hall. The military postings led to Bruce being born in Aldershot and he always sounded more Home Counties than Scottish as he produced his articulate comments on the game. He was big and strong, with a ferocious shot in his left foot. Mackay deployed him in the inside-right channel, which enabled Rioch to cut across defenders and let fly. He made his debut in a 4-2 victory over Norwich City at Carrow Road, a game that provided an important pointer to different thinking at Derby. Clough and Taylor would have been furious that Norwich were given two goals after the Rams dominated: Mackay did not bother, on the grounds that Derby had four. Considering all that happened, it was a major achievement for Derby to finish third, although well behind Leeds and Liverpool, to win a place in the UEFA Cup. It even washed away the memory of a chaotic annual meeting in December. As this was called to consider the previous financial year, there was no need to field questions about the resignations of Clough and Taylor but the Protest Movement, having spread their shares around, were not inclined to miss the opportunity and Longson swallowed the hook. He threatened to have opponents thrown out and chucked down the stairs, slandered a builder who then turned up to complain and, in one unforgettable moment, tried to talk with the microphone at his ear. Mike Carey, covering the event for *The Guardian*, wrote it up as a pantomime, with Longson in the role of Baron Notsohardup. It was a complete shambles and Mackay, rather than the occupants of the boardroom, forced the football world to take Derby County seriously again.

As he knew when he took the job, Mackay did not have to make many changes to the team, although one was forced on him when, playing for England against Northern Ireland in May, 1974, Roy McFarland tore an Achilles tendon and was out of contention until the following April. The only major arrival in summer was Francis Lee, £100,000 from Manchester City, and the *Evening Telegraph* received a letter from one of the many manifestations of Mr K.N.Owall, saying that, at 30, Lee was finished. There was a malicious pleasure in returning it, without comment, to the sender eight months later. Lee had already faced that issue: "Here, I could win anything," he said, "Cup medals, a UEFA Cup medal or another League Championship. Everybody thinks that, because I'm 30, I'm ready to be shot. You can be a good striker at 28 but two years later everyone thinks you're finished. I don't see that at all." Lee, already running his own waste paper conversion company, played on because he wanted to: he was financially secure and, as a player never short of confidence, brought a swagger to the club, rather as Mackay had in 1968. Before 1974-75 started, my preview suggested that Derby were a better bet for Cups than the League because they could lack consistency. That remained true but the First Division was so tight that the lead changed hands frequently, with Carlisle United the first to show, and nobody was good enough to dominate. In the end, it boiled down to timing as Derby produced a good run at the right time, eight victories from 10 games in March and April. Nobody could answer that and Derby collected the Championship trophy before their final home game, against Carlisle. For much of the season, that was an unlikely outcome. Derby were away slowly, only one win in the first seven matches, and remained patchy past the turn of the year. There were enough good moments to keep them in touch, such as Peter Daniel's first goal in a 4-1 defeat of Chelsea in September. Early forecasts were that McFarland would be back in the New Year, so Mackay trusted his available options. Thomas was one but was injured in a pre-season game, so Daniel embarked on the greatest season of his life. He was a product of Tim Ward's Sunday trials and, under Clough and Taylor, cast as a utility defender who could come in anywhere across the back although, to his disappointment, Daniel never figured in the 1971-72 Championship. The idea that a player is effective for only a limited number of games is common and often means he never has the run to prove differently. Given the chance, Daniel demonstrated he was perfectly capable of going through a season at the top level and he ended as Player of the Year as Colin Todd, already the Professional Footballers' Association Player of the Year, gave what was effectively a casting vote following a dead heat so that

Daniel could enjoy the praise. It was more probably an ordeal as Daniel hated being the centre of attention. Mackay's instinct was always to attack but beating Leeds at Elland Road by virtue of an heroic defensive display gave Derby as much satisfaction as any result. Powell, standing in for the injured Todd, had much to do with it before Lee poked a late winner over David Harvey. Powell was unlucky not to have featured more in the second Championship but an injury early in the season let in Newton, who played well enough to retain the place and show why Clough and Taylor were so keen to sign him. In the next game, Kevin Hector scored a hat-trick as Queen's Park Rangers were swept aside but consistency remained elusive.

That flaw was evident in the UEFA Cup. After a comfortable victory over the Geneva team Servette, Derby eliminated Atletico Madrid, European Cup Finalists in 1974, on penalties after two tremendous games. In the confined area outside the dressing-rooms in Madrid, Juan Carlos Lorenzo, who coached Argentina's 1966 World Cup team, seized on Archie Gemmill, grasped him in a bear-hug and bellowed 'Gemmill magnifico.' The Rams carried a 3-1 lead to Yugoslavia but contrived to lose to Velez Mostar and, just before Christmas, were beaten by bottom club Luton Town at Kenilworth Road. They stood 10th that night but so compressed was the League that they were only five points behind that week's leaders, Ipswich Town. Derby had a chance of finishing in a good position but so did half the First Division. Lee was given a good reception when he returned to Maine Road and responded with a splendid goal that gained a kind of immortality when Barry Davies, commentating for *Match of the Day*, suddenly hurtled up through the octaves in his excitement. "Look at his face, just look at his face." It is still given an occasional airing almost 30 years on. Powell scored twice when Derby beat Arsenal, who had Alan Ball and Bob McNab sent off for dissent, and the push finally started at the beginning of March. Tottenham Hotspur were beaten at the Baseball Ground and Chelsea at Stamford Bridge before a blip at home. At that stage, the pitch was an area of clinging mud and after Stoke City's victory, Alan Hudson was asked if he ever played on a worse surface. "Only once," he said, "for England Under-23 against Scotland at Derby." Mackay took it in his stride: "We'll just have to win at Newcastle," he said and so they did, with a clever goal from David Nish and a surge of power from Bruce Rioch. The score with Luton was settled when the Easter rush began as Roger Davies scored all the goals in a 5-0 victory. He looked more incredulous as his tally mounted and could have had more. "If it had been his day, Roger could have scored 10," said Mackay but he was the first to bag five in a game for Derby since Hughie Gallacher at Blackburn in December, 1934. Derby hit another five at Burnley on Easter Monday with their most compelling display of the season and as I drove away from Turf Moor with the photographer, we stopped to give a lift to a Burnley supporter. "If they play like that away, what on earth are they like at home?" he asked. The instant answer, the following day, is that they were made to work hard before Rioch's two goals beat Manchester City but they had maximum points over Easter to draw level with Ipswich and Everton. The title was on, they were the team in form and were convinced that fate was with them when they salvaged a draw at Middlesbrough, Hector's late equaliser stemming from the way Gemmill worried Stuart Boam into losing possession. Jack Charlton was furious and Alan Hinton said: "It looks as if we are meant to win the title." Hinton came into the team when Lee was injured and, at a vital time, gave a new shape to the attack, backed by his experience from the first title. McFarland returned for the last four games, just at the right time as Daniel was enduring increasing discomfort from a pelvic injury. Gemmill retained the captaincy because there was enough pressure on the centre-half after 11 months out of senior football. Class will out and he played a significant part in narrow home wins over Wolves and West Ham. When Derby settled for 0-0 in an untidy game at Leicester, it looked like a useful point but within minutes of the final whistle, the dressing-room was bouncing. Everton and Liverpool lost, so only Ipswich could deprive Derby of the title. In 1972, it was settled when the players were in Majorca: this time they were closer, in a Derby nightclub for the Awards Night presentations. Manchester City held Ipswich to a draw while the prizes were handed out and Derby were Champions for the second time in four seasons. For the first time as a manager, Mackay began and ended a season at the same club. Before it started, he said he wanted to be judged on what he achieved and here was the perfect answer.

He happily shared the credit with his assistant, Des Anderson, who accompanied him from Nottingham Forest. They had known each other for years and laughed easily. Anderson had, as he admitted, no claim to be a tactical genius but saw his role as keeping everybody in the right frame of mind to give of their best. Like Mackay, he believed in good players being allowed to express themselves. The atmosphere was more free and easy than under Clough and Taylor but the principles were not that different – find skill in every department. Jimmy Gordon followed Clough to Leeds, then the City Ground, so Gordon Guthrie was the physio. This great Derby loyalist first played in the junior sides and Reserves under Harry Storer but never appeared in the first team. He moved towards coaching and physiotherapy, serving a succession of managers. Whether they were good or bad, all found a loyal ally in Guthrie and were confident that he kept everything inside the club. There is a great book in Guth but he will never write or allow it to be written because it would mean breaking confidences, which is why players as well as managers have so much respect for him.

Throughout 1974-75, Todd maintained an incredibly high standard. The PFA Award indicated the opinion of other professionals and it remains the best individual season I ever saw. It is possible that, with McFarland absent, Todd felt it necessary to assume greater responsibility but the essence of his game was so simple. He was at the back to win the ball and move it on to another Derby player. Todd was so hard to beat because his strength was backed by pace, so opponents who thought they had escaped found him coming back for another bite. In terms of influence, Gemmill was little behind him as his driving energy in midfield meant he led by example. He missed only one match and, although he did not score all season, was central to everything. The midfield goals came from Rioch, whose 15 made him the leading scorer in the League. Hector and Lee contributed 25 between them but, as in 1971-72, success stemmed from the balance of the team. An injury to Webster finally let in Thomas, who was able to show why Mackay signed him from Swindon. He, too, was hard to escape, with a long leg coming round for a recovery tackle. Nish was as elegant as any player ever to appear for Derby and, having sealed the title, Derby completed their fixtures at home to Carlisle, by then relegated after their early burst. Before the start, there was a parade of old players, an event originally designed to mark the end of the pitch. Mud caused so many problems and the surface was dug up in summer, with capsules of earth sold as souvenirs. It needed to be done but, in succeeding years, everything possible went wrong with the playing area. Derby hardly finished with a flourish, a 0-0 draw confirming that Championship celebrations had continued almost up to kick-off time.

As manager of the Champions in summer, 1975, Mackay was under no pressure to buy and was prepared to make a move only if he became aware of a player certain to add something to a talented side. He was on holiday in Scotland when, in July, there was talk of Charlie George crossing North London from Arsenal to Tottenham Hotspur. A hint was enough for Mackay to book the next available flight and he beat his old club to sign George for £100,000. Although £1-million deals were a few years away, the fee felt like daylight robbery on Mackay's part. George, a member of Arsenal's 1970-71 double team, was a hero at Highbury and, at 24, had his peak years ahead. He had an image problem, with his long hair and an apparently rebellious attitude that provoked frequent disputes with authority, so I wondered if professional relationships would be fraught. As it turned out, there was never a cross word, although it helped to be friendly with his then wife Susan, assumed by Sam Longson to be the actress of the same name. He savoured the atmosphere on a pre-season tour to Scotland. "Just look at the gaffer," he said on the team bus, "joking and larking about. I never saw Bertie Mee [his manager at Highbury] with a smile on his face." It was a relaxed trip, with guarantees from matches against Celtic, the Champions, and Hibernian struggling to keep pace with the Edinburgh hotel bill as Mackay's old friends came calling. All George wanted was to play in the right environment, among others who knew what they were doing, and he was sensational that season, from his debut in the Charity Shield to the moment he dislocated a shoulder the following March. Even now, he raises the roof on the occasions he walks out on the pitch to greet supporters, so great was his impact at Derby. West Ham United, victors over Fulham in a terminally dull Cup Final, were beaten at

Wembley through goals from Hector and McFarland, although the lavish Championship dinner at the London Hilton in Park Lane, following the Charity Shield date, worried a few senior players. "Recognition from the club is nice," said McFarland, "but we should be getting on with the new season." There was another tilt at the European Cup for a start but, despite one of the great Baseball Ground nights, they were out before Christmas. They came back from a 1-0 defeat in Czechoslovakia to beat Slovan Bratislava, with Jeff Bourne adding to Lee's two goals. Bourne, who came from Linton, near Burton-upon-Trent, had few chances under Clough and Taylor: it was, of course, hard for a forward to push past O'Hare and Hector, who were seldom absent, but Mackay found that Bourne could hold the ball, beat a man and score a few goals. It set him off on a fair career, with Crystal Palace and Sheffield United as well as several clubs in the United States. Real Madrid were next for one of the greatest occasions in Derby's history. The first leg at the Baseball Ground started brilliantly when George ran diagonally at Gemmill's low centre and thrashed a left-footed shot past Miguel Angel. It was the first of a hat-trick, the others coming from penalties, and Nish also scored as Derby won 4-1. Todd and Gemmill were supreme against the greatest of all European Cup clubs and where once such a fixture was hard to imagine, in 1975 it was the outcome that was the startling aspect. Real had a goal ruled out for offside and the wielder of the flag compelled a second glance. The officials were from the Soviet Union and it was indeed Tewfik Bakhramov, still a linesman nine years after his momentous over-the-line decision, for Geoff Hurst's second goal in the Wembley World Cup Final. Ten days later, Derby suffered a crucial blow in the process of beating Leeds 3-2 at the Baseball Ground as Lee and Norman Hunter engaged in their notorious, if memorable, clash. It began when Hunter fouled Lee and George converted the penalty. Even with a chance to gather himself during the interval, Hunter was still simmering and clattered into Lee seven minutes into the second half. Lee reacted to the late challenge, and was then punched on the top lip by Hunter, causing a split that required four stitches. Derek Nippard sent off both players and, as Lee told it, there was a gap where his lip should have been while he had not even landed a blow. Halfway to the touchline, he did something about it and round two was an old-fashioned street brawl. Billy Bremner was the most disappointed man after pecking round the edges without becoming fully involved. There were some afters in the corridor outside the dressing-rooms and a nasty taste lingering, although Davies won a storming game with his late goal. As domestic suspensions then spread to European games, Lee was out of the return in Madrid. Rioch was injured, McFarland and Newton far from full fitness. McFarland, indeed, had a public injection in the dug-out, administered with an implement that looked as if it had been borrowed from a local vet, before the start of extra-time but played astonishingly well on one leg. George hit a stunning goal and Derby, although overwhelmed, were close to safety until Real's brilliant captain, Amancio, went down as Thomas challenged to earn a penalty. It looked totally unconvincing but the Swiss referee had 120,000 screaming at him to give it. Santillana put away the fifth to clinch the tie but it was hard on George, with four goals over the two legs. After that mauling, Derby did remarkably well to beat Arsenal three days later, even if it left the Highbury crowd even more tetchy about the sale of George, who was greeted with a bouquet of flowers from his mates on the North Bank terrace. At the end of November, Mackay signed Leighton James from Burnley for £300,000 but, for all his powerful pace, the Welsh winger found it hard to hit a consistent streak. Derby went well though and, by early March, had a chance of the double. They beat Everton, Liverpool, Southend and Newcastle in successive home FA Cup ties while maintaining their League form. Injuries forced Newcastle to pick third choice Eddie Edgar in goal but Rioch's second, a free kick, would have beaten anybody. "The ball hit the net and came out the other side as chips," said Des Anderson, who liked to mull over his one-liners before revealing them. George's injury put him out of the Hillsborough semi-final and Gordon Hill's two goals won it for Manchester United but it was only 1-0 when, as he had planned, David Nish beat the offside trap. Under Tommy Docherty, United were always quick to push up but Nish collected the ball, chipped it over the rushing defenders and strode through. Even before he beat Alex Stepney, the whistle went for offside against forwards trying to come back. Even before modern interpretations of active and inactive, it was a wretched decision by Jack Taylor and a moment that suggested Derby were doomed. After that, the season tailed away sadly until Lee marked his 500th and final League game before retirement with two late goals in a 6-2 victory over Ipswich at Portman Road. To Bobby Robson's distress, Ipswich appeared to think the season ended a week earlier but Derby's was extended into the small hours by Lee's farewell drinks party in King's Lynn. The travelling director, Sydney Bradley, found it impossible to persuade anybody to return to the coach. Despite only one win in the last five games, Derby were fourth and in Europe again.

Davies was sold to Bruges in summer, Lee finished and Bourne was on loan to Dallas Tornado in the North American Soccer League, so Derby were short of forwards when they played their pre-season games. Hinton, too, had left, full of praise for the support and sympathy Mackay gave him during the fatal illness of his son Matthew. That worry, along with business problems, meant Hinton was hardly involved in 1975-76 but he built a successful new career in the United States, as a player, then a coach. He was still good enough to set an NASL record for assists when he was with Vancouver Whitecaps and the family eventually made a home in Seattle. Mackay wanted to sign Trevor Francis but there was little encouragement from his own board, whatever Birmingham City may have thought, so Derby made a poor start with a patched-up attack. A UEFA Cup tie against Finn Harps from the Republic of Ireland allowed them to set a club record in a 12-0 victory at the Baseball Ground, five goals to Hector, but there was no win in the first eight League games, until something as spectacular happened. Rioch, used as an emergency striker, hit four as Tottenham, even with Pat Jennings in goal, were hammered 8-2. That failed to quieten the criticism and rumours which reached their peak a fortnight earlier when, following a verbal transfer request from Todd, Derby were awful in a 5-1 defeat by Birmingham. There was, too, a new element on the board and, at the annual meeting, vice-chairman George Hardy smoothly took over when Longson struggled for words: nothing new about that. Hardy would have stayed quiet had he realised how bitterly Longson was to view the intervention. Golf club chatter, always a good conduit for passing opinions to directors, was running against Mackay and, ignoring advice, he sought a vote of confidence. As Derby finished third, first and fourth, as well as reaching their first FA Cup semi-final for 28 years, it was hardly unreasonable to ask for support but it was not forthcoming, so Mackay and Anderson were sacked. Like Clough and Taylor, they lasted 18 months after lifting the Championship trophy, emphasising the truth that Derby County are totally unable to handle success. At the very least, Mackay and Anderson should have been given time to resolve the problem, which was less daunting than succeeding Clough and Taylor in such a fraught atmosphere. Instead, Colin Murphy, the Reserve team coach brought in by Mackay, was appointed caretaker. Murphy, with a non-League background as a player, was an energetic coach and later, as Lincoln City manager, produced a programme column so opaque as to achieve cult status: or, as he once remarked in a television interview, "I think that's what they're saying." Within a fortnight, Bruce Rioch was sold to Everton and Derby spent more than £300,000 to bring centre-forward Derek Hales from Charlton Athletic. Murphy spoke of Hales and Charlie George as the best striking combination in the League but the evidence never justified the claim. George, devastated by Mackay's departure, failed to blend with the new man. Hales, used to the open spaces at the Valley, really needed his former partner Mike Flanagan and two wingers to be effective but doubts about the signing did not prevent Murphy being appointed on a full-time basis in January, 1977, and promptly engaging Dario Gradi as his assistant. Gradi, an intelligent man, went on to establish himself in a long career as manager of Crewe Alexandra, during which he gave a perfect demonstration of how to handle a club of limited financial resources. On the surface, it appeared they were being given every chance but supporters remained unconvinced and some on the board had entirely different plans. In February, Derby sought permission from Nottingham Forest to approach Brian Clough and Peter Taylor, aiming to restore them at the Baseball Ground. Talks at George Hardy's house seemed to go well, although it was later clear that the financial offer was not sufficiently tempting. The day after the story became public, sparking a rush on tickets for the FA Cup fifth round tie against Blackburn Rovers, journalists waited for the great reunion. Confidence at the Baseball Ground began to falter as time passed and died when a statement was issued at the City Ground by Forest vice-chairman Stuart Dryden. Even so, Clough appeared, driven by Jimmy Gordon and accompanied by Vince Wilson, a journalist friend from the North-East. Wilson went into the boardroom at one end and straight out of the other, with Murphy peering out of his office door as the situation developed. Derby's directors were already stunned: mouths sagged and Adam's apples jumped when the Forest statement was read to them: Clough came only to deliver his reasons in person.

The coup exploded in Derby's faces and, having digested failure, they turned again to Murphy. If he thought that was poor treatment, his end at Derby would be handled with even less dignity. For the time being, he was back on duty, had a new chairman in Hardy as the board eased out Longson and soon signed Gerry Daly from Manchester United for £170,000. Not that Longson was finished because, after defeat by West Bromwich Albion increased relegation fears, he went public to say that Mackay should be reinstated. It was open warfare between Longson, now president, and the new chairman, who accused him of: "Mischief making and hypocrisy and talking dangerous and dishonest rubbish." Poor Murphy was caught in the crossfire and nothing he encountered in the future as a manager could surprise him after the Derby experience. The Cup dream ended with defeat by Everton at Goodison Park and at least relegation was avoided, owing something to a meeting the players held in private. The edifice was rocking and after six League games of the following season, Murphy was out of a job. He sat and watched a 2-2 draw with Leeds United while aware that Tommy Docherty was on his way to be announced as the new manager. The lack of sensitivity was hard to credit and, not for the last time, Derby County was regarded as a joke club. Docherty was available because, after winning the FA Cup with Manchester United, he was dismissed over an affair with the wife of physiotherapist Laurie Brown. Docherty embarked on 20 months of buying and selling that seriously diminished the quality on the field. Changes were needed but not for their own sake. Colin Boulton, Colin Todd, Archie Gemmill, Kevin Hector, Charlie George and Leighton James were among the departures while, of all Docherty's signings, only Steve Buckley proved a long-term investment. He brought Rioch back from Everton and James went to Queen's Park Rangers in an exchange involving Don Masson. Daly made up a midfield trio and Docherty said: "Come and see my three Van Goghs." I remember asking Frank Blunstone, Docherty's assistant, which of the artists planned to win the ball. "That's a job for the defenders," said Blunstone who, although a thoroughly pleasant man, did not endear himself by wearing a Manchester United tracksuit at Raynesway. Masson, 31 when he arrived, was hugely unpopular with fans in his season at Derby. He went with Scotland to Argentina for the 1978 World Cup and there were tales of contemptuous cheers in Derby pubs when he missed a penalty against Iran. James left at the age of 24 and the £300,000 fee that shifted him from Burnley effectively dwindled to nothing when Masson returned to Notts County as a swap for Steve Carter. And after all his achievements for Derby, it was surely not necessary to name Hector as substitute for the Reserves to hasten him on his way to Vancouver Whitecaps. Although Docherty had a sharp Glaswegian wit, he was liable to tread on anybody in his way and also had to negotiate a failed court action, having accused a former Manchester United player, Willie Morgan, of libel. Docherty could fill newspapers and kept Derby in the First Division before leaving for a second spell at Queen's Park Rangers. But the slide was on and chaos continued in the boardroom. Perhaps the most depressing aspect, looking back over the years, is the total inability to learn from previous mistakes: for as long as boardroom feuds persist, effective leadership is impossible, so players and managers work in an unhelpful atmosphere. Hardy tried to create a stable situation but had to reach accommodation with John Kirkland, son of Jack and a major shareholder, who expressed concern about the running of the club. Colin Addison, who had been assistant to Ron Atkinson at West Brom, succeeded Docherty and persuaded John Newman to leave his job as manager of Grimsby Town to assist him. They negotiated with Hardy, who lost his position when the board decided to revert to a two-yearly change of chairman. At the pre-season photograph, it was like musical chairs as everybody waited to see who would occupy the middle seat. Richard Moore, an accountant who ran the hosiery firm Cox Moore in Long Eaton, took it and, with

Derby's finances already ailing, proceeded to make them worse. They soon lost Stuart Webb as general secretary. He was suspended in summer, soon after police moved in to investigate financial affairs at the Baseball Ground, and resigned in August, 1978, to develop his successful Lonsdale Travel business. Michael Dunford, a supporter long before he started work in the offices, took over as secretary. Nor was Longson entirely spent, because Hardy's continued presence on the board rankled. The next annual meeting saw to that although, following a deferment because of the police investigation, it did not take place until January, 1980. Hardy and Bob Innes, a Derby estate agent who had been his vice-chairman, were swept away and with relegation the most likely outcome on the field, there were rocky times ahead. Before the UEFA Cup game against AEK Athens, I stood near the Parthenon with Barrie Eccleston, then the Rams man for Radio Derby, and talked about seeing everywhere in Europe if we stuck with the club. Some judges we were.

TEARS AT LORD'S

ONLY twice in 32 years did I feel emotionally involved in events. The first occasion was Derby County's decision to accept the resignations of Brian Clough and Peter Taylor, an act betraying not only stupidity but a self-defeating malice. Derbyshire's victory in the 1981 NatWest Trophy Final was my most memorable day in journalism, largely because the County Cricket Club spent years striving to survive rather than thinking about winning anything. The arrival of Eddie Barlow revived morale and increased commitment so, although he had left by then, the day at Lord's owed something to him. It was probably Mike Carey's suggestion that, in the troubled 1970s, Derbyshire should liaise with the English Tourist Board and turn the annual change of captaincy into a ceremony to attract cricket followers from around the world. It happened in mid-season often enough for the weather to be reasonable enough for the trippers but was inevitably linked to poor results. In four seasons, from 1971 to 1974, Derbyshire were bottom of the Championship three times and rose by only one place in the other year. In 1975 and 1976, they were 15th, in the days before Durham became the 18th county, so the struggle was long and often dispiriting. Grim it may have been but there were always players worth watching. Throughout this time, Derbyshire had one of the best wicketkeepers in the world, Bob Taylor, quietly demonstrating his quality while Mike Hendrick and Geoff Miller developed into England cricketers, even if Alan Ward, who beat them to Test recognition, was unable to fulfil his early potential. There were enough others of county class to put together a better team but the parts never fitted into a satisfactory whole, so the leadership had to be questioned, on and off the field. In preparation for their centenary year, Derbyshire engaged the former England bowler Fred Rumsey as commercial manager but in 1971, when they hoped to raise enough money to end immediate financial worries, they contrived to make less than in an average year. Rumsey's major contribution was as a one-day bowler who helped them to reach the 1969 Gillette Cup Final, in which they were comprehensively beaten by Yorkshire. At the time, the County Ground was, by some distance, the bleakest headquarters on the circuit, with no pavilion, inadequate dressing-rooms and the constant threat of a wind which, when the mood took it, whipped down the old Racecourse. Lunches, served in the depths of the Grandstand, did not merit gourmet status and a number of players organised an alternative run to a nearby transport café. For two years, between the opening matches of 1975 and 1977, Derbyshire did not play at the County Ground, preferring to take their matches round the county following a disagreement with their landlords, the Council. Around the same time, they scrapped the Second team for financial reasons. Derbyshire were poor relations and lived down to the part.

Ian Buxton resigned the captaincy in 1972, although he played for a further year, and Brian Bolus was engaged from Nottinghamshire for the following season. By May, 1975, Bolus had run out of conflicting theories on how the game should be played and handed the baton to Taylor. It was never likely to succeed because Taylor was a perfectionist about his work behind the stumps, so anything interfering with that was an unwelcome distraction. Taylor was like another Staffordshire man who had a shot at leading Derbyshire, David Steele: when they arrived in a morning, they were perfectly prepared for the day ahead and simply could not understand others who needed to be cajoled or organised. As a result, both found captaincy a burden but at least help was at hand for Taylor. In what was then a rare moment of inspiration, Derbyshire engaged the South African Barlow for 1976, with a three-year contract. Here was a man with the status and personality to lift a club that was desperate for a change of image. Barlow did exactly what was hoped but, when he left, Derbyshire took another backward leap. Steele, brought from Northamptonshire to replace Barlow as captain for 1979, lasted only until July, when Miller took over and was in turn a mid-season casualty in 1981. This time, Barry Wood stepped up and was an immediate success with victory in the NatWest Trophy, Derbyshire's first major prize since the 1936 Championship. Even that did not guarantee Wood a long and happy tenure as Kim Barnett succeeded him in May, 1983. Eight captains in 12 years is a statistic saying everything about Derbyshire of this period because, without stability, it was a poor environment for players and supporters. Behind this, there were too many committee and administrative changes. Given all the circumstances, it is remarkable that a peak was scaled so memorably at Lord's. Barlow was 35 when he arrived in Derbyshire and, although his best days were inevitably behind him, remained a bustling, influential all-rounder. In the early part of his career, he was part of a South African team that could have ruled world cricket had their government's apartheid policy not led to a lengthy ban from international competition. In 1968, English cricket ran into political trouble by omitting Basil D'Oliveira from their team to tour South Africa. D'Oliveira, a Cape Coloured from South Africa, was worth a place, especially after his 158 against Australia at the Oval. Cricket followers in this country sensed a scarcely hidden agenda and the situation became worse when Tom Cartwright withdrew and D'Oliveira was named as a replacement, illogically a batsman in place of a bowler. The South African Prime Minister, John Vorster, said he would not accept a team containing D'Oliveira and the tour was cancelled as, in turn, was South Africa's scheduled visit to England in 1970. There was a fear of direct action by anti-apartheid groups, who would have brought chaos to Test grounds, so a Rest of the World side, containing Barlow, overwhelmed England in five excellent games, later ruled not to be Test matches. South Africa's temporary obituary remained a spanking 4-0 victory over Australia but at least Barlow had something approaching a Test career, with 30 appearances. For Barry Richards, an unarguably great batsman as he demonstrated for Hampshire, the four Tests against Australia were the beginning and end, but still four more than Clive Rice, an inspiration to Nottinghamshire, managed. A Test batting average of 45.74 established Barlow's credentials, so he did not travel to England to prove anything, rather to add a competitive edge to his cricket. For a time, he struggled for consistent runs, although the Rutland Ground at Ilkeston suited him. He scored a century against Nottinghamshire there and, after assuming the captaincy, a resplendent 217 in a victory over Surrey. The determination he added was evident in August, when Derbyshire beat Lancashire at Buxton after following on. There was no obvious improvement in the record for 1975 but there were signs of a changed mood, raising hope that there could be a parallel with the arrival of Brian Clough and Peter Taylor at the Baseball Ground. Barlow's influence was evident in his bowling because, like Derbyshire's first overseas player of modern times, Chris Wilkins, he expected to take a wicket with every ball. Barlow was a more distinguished player than his fellow South African, although Wilkins performed a remarkable feat by dismissed Zaheer Abbas, the elegant Pakistan and Gloucestershire batsman, twice in a match, once bowling right-arm medium as usual and the second time trying some left-arm slow. The Barlow bark of 'Watch' when Derbyshire were fielding was constantly heard and he was often seen in individual net sessions, memorably when urging Alan Hill to go through with his strokes.

Hill, who once scored a century for Orange Free State without a single boundary during a winter contract, was always inclined to be obdurate as a batsman but served Derbyshire outstandingly well in a number of roles, coach and temporary secretary as well as an opening batsman whose courage was never more graphically proved than in a century against Hampshire, including the great Malcolm Marshall, despite what turned out to be a cracked kneecap. Mention of the notable OFS century always brought the same response from Hill: "Who won the game, then?" He flourished under Barlow, as did Geoff Miller who, given extra responsibility, moved towards his first Test. Others fared less well. Fred Swarbrook, a left-arm spinner who took nine for 20 against Sussex at Hove in 1975 and was also a gritty batsman, found his confidence undermined by Barlow's demands. In later years, he lost his bowling completely, as Roger Finney was to do, and it was agony watching as they hardly dared to let the ball go. A psychologist suggested that Swarbrook should carry a smooth stone in his pocket and rub it for reassurance. During another clenched spell, against Lancashire at Aigburth, Steele called across: "Why not put the ball in your pocket, Fred, and send down the pebble?" Only strong minds could cope with Barlow and, while there is no doubt that Derbyshire improved while he was with them, there was little in the way of a permanent legacy. Something similar applied when he returned to England as Gloucestershire coach and propelled young players into the county game. They were fine while he was there but later appeared to wonder what they were doing in first-class cricket. It is possible that Barlow was too powerful a character, with a faith in his own ability that made it hard for him to understand more fragile egos. With the addition of one player, New Zealand left-hander John Wright, Derbyshire rose to seventh in the 1977 Championship through playing confident, aggressive cricket. Barlow was at his best as captain and, in 1978, they reached the Final of the Benson and Hedges Cup. By the time they arrived at Lord's, the impetus that lasted for one-and-a-half seasons was fading, as injuries bit, and they were comfortably beaten by Kent. Derbyshire's 147, after deciding to bat, was well short of requirements and all hope disappeared when Bob Woolmer, on his way to the Gold Award, was twice dropped off successive balls from Mike Hendrick. As the culprits were Barlow and Bob Taylor, the two men Derbyshire followers would have backed to hold anything, it was clearly not their day. In the previous year, Derbyshire alarmed Second XI opposition by including Peter Kirsten and Allan Lamb, two of Barlow's Western Province proteges. They opted for Kirsten, so Lamb moved on to a considerable career with Northamptonshire and England. The combination of Wright and Kirsten produced a vintage period for Derbyshire batting. Wright played in 82 Tests for New Zealand and was their highest aggregate scorer until overtaken by Martin Crowe, so his county appearances depended on international calls. South Africa were then in exile and Kirsten was constantly available for five seasons. The readmission to the international game was just in time for Kirsten, who was then 36, and it was an emotional moment for Derbyshire followers when he hit 104 against England at Headingley in 1994. Steele used to call him 'the Don' because he resembled Sir Don Bradman in stature, Derbyshire then wore Australian-style baggy caps and, perhaps most of all, Kirsten was destructive once set. He scored six double hundreds for Derbyshire and set a county record in 1982 with eight centuries. At the start of an innings, he played so quietly that spectators hardly registered until they began to wonder how he had reached 30: in later stages, especially when he was into three figures, every ball was compelling, so vivid were his strokes, some apparently created on the spur of the moment. In 1980 when, in one of the periodic fiddles with the regulations, first innings were limited to 100 overs, Kirsten destroyed the Glamorgan attack in an unbeaten 213. He hit 32 fours and five sixes but most remarkable was his complete domination as he added the last 105 out of 127 in only 18 overs, finishing with 63 from the last seven.

An entirely different kind of innings in the same summer typified Wright. Derbyshire met the West Indian tourists at Queen's Park in May and, naturally, wanted as placid a pitch as possible in view of the available fast bowlers preparing for the Test series. As Queen's Park is publicly owned, the Council had a say, so decided that the pitch looked drab and should be freshened with a late watering. Because Barry Wood left Lancashire immediately after a testimonial raising in excess of £62,000, he was barred from the Championship until June 1 but was eligible for a debut against the tourists. Before going out to face Andy Roberts and Malcolm Marshall, Wood left a confident message in the dressing-room, instructing the 12th man to have his floppy hat ready to exchange for a helmet once he had seen off the new ball. On a surface that soon proved dangerous, Wood was hit on the side of the head by a ball from Roberts in the opening over and retired, dazed and bleeding. While Wood sat recovering, Steele, who always addressed him as Nathan, could not resist the quip. "Here's your floppy, Nathan. You can use it to wipe off the blood." Although Michael Holding was not involved in the game, it was a fearsome attack, with Joel Garner and Collis King to back the new-ball pair. Wright did not give an inch and his 96 remains one of the bravest innings I ever saw, matched for a time on the day by Steele's courage. The Council's Leisure director was not the most popular man around and Mike

Hendrick's hat-trick to end the West Indians' innings was not greeted with wholehearted enthusiasm. It merely meant that his victims, Marshall, Roberts and Garner, could be about their business that much earlier. Wright's implacable determination was masked by a delightfully vague personality that gave him the air of a permanent student. He was known as Shake in the dressing-room, apparently from his habit of arriving for the start of a season and emptying his bag on the floor to see what kit fell out. Once, having trouble with his grip, he stuck his right batting glove to the bat handle with superglue. This, he reasoned, would keep his top hand in position but when it worked to the extent of a long innings, he began to realise that the perspiration could mean his hand was also permanently attached. In bad times, notably three ducks in a weekend at Chelmsford, he smiled ruefully but it was always clear that he would put it right. He was back in Derby in 2002, as a successful and popular coach to a good Indian side. When he came round for a chat, we asked what he had done to make the Indians, notoriously weak once they left home, more competitive. Wright said his main function was to keep an eye on the practice balls. "It's a nightmare, mate," he said. "If you don't watch it, they just disappear." The same John Wright but his captain, Sourav Ganguly, had a high opinion of his capabilities, not least in the way he relaxed players to allow them to give their best.

Wood, who was 37 when he joined Derbyshire, marked his return to Championship cricket with a century at Edgbaston and remained a competitive player. He opened the batting, was a fine close fielder and, especially in one-day games, a valuable bowler with his wobbling seam. It was the style Philip Russell, the coach for many years after his playing days, termed heavy water. By way of explanation, he said: "The ball drifts down and, just when you think of hitting it out of the ground, you find it sticks to your bat." Wood was an irritating opponent, especially with his yelped appeals, but a good man to have in any camp. He was always keen to lead a county and, although one of those who dissuaded Geoff Miller from resigning in the first half of 1981, took up the challenge in July when Miller repeated his request to stand down. Six weeks later, he held up the inaugural NatWest Trophy, Gillette's 18-year sponsorship having come to a close. Derbyshire began with a comfortable victory over Suffolk at Bury St Edmunds and beat Worcestershire over two days at New Road in the second round. Colin Tunnicliffe turned the game with five for 15 in four overs, limiting Worcestershire, who had been 199 for five, to 228 from their 60 overs on a slow pitch, leaving Kirsten to steer them through on the reserve day. The captaincy changed hands before the quarter-final and the home game against Nottinghamshire was the first of three tense occasions. Derbyshire were without Hendrick and Miller and, on another slow pitch, their total of 164 looked inadequate, more so when Nottinghamshire reached 75 for one in the 28th over. Then Wood and Steele shared four wickets in the space of 10 overs, also stifling the runs, to give Derbyshire a grip they never released. Richard Hadlee tried to break out and hit Steele for 14 in one over but the left-arm spinner's other 11 cost only nine. It was at this time that Paul Newman began to attract attention as a young English bowler with genuine pace, something that always alerted the selectors. He spent a decade with Derbyshire but did not fulfil early potential: a sound county performer rather than one who could step up to international level. If victory over Nottinghamshire tested the nerves, Derbyshire followers came to look back on it as a gentle stroll. The semi-final against Essex put them through the shredder and the Final was a repeat. The County Ground pitch in the semi-final was tailored for seam bowlers and, provided they found the right areas, fast scoring was virtually impossible, neither side managing two-and-a-half an over. The prized Essex wicket for most of his 25 years was that of Graham Gooch and Newman removed him cheaply, through one of Taylor's six catches. Ken McEwan, another danger, was run out but Norbert Phillip hit a useful 42. Essex's 149 was hardly formidable but Derbyshire knew every run would have to be earned off John Lever, Phillip, Derek Pringle and Stuart Turner. Kim Barnett, not long turned 21, showed the temperament that was to make him one of Derbyshire's great players with an invaluable 59 but it boiled towards an agonising finish, 40 required from the last 10 overs, 11 to win or 10 to tie from the final one, Phillip to bowl. Newman and Taylor, who came off at the end with strain etched on his face, scuttled for everything until Newman pulled the fifth ball for four. That meant

Derbyshire needed one run from the last ball to draw level and go through by virtue of losing fewer wickets. Newman made contact and sprinted, Phillip followed through to pick up the ball. A gentle throw to Brian Hardie, already over the stumps at the bowler's end, would have been enough but Phillip went for a direct hit. He missed the stumps as well, fortunately, as Hardie, Newman was home and Derbyshire on their way to Lord's. Phillip was distraught but, in an instinctive moment of true leadership, the Essex captain Keith Fletcher immediately put an arm round his shoulder. Essex were a popular, as well as a very good, side in those years because they played hard, then enjoyed themselves. They were quick to congratulate Derbyshire and wish them well against Northamptonshire, who beat Lancashire by one wicket with a ball to spare before settling in front of their television sets to see the conclusion from Derby on the second day. The new sponsors were delighted with the interest generated by two remarkable semi-finals but hardly dared hope for anything like that in the Final.

Cricket usually gave way to football on my working schedule when the seasons overlapped but there was no contest on September 5, 1981. There was only a cringe when the results came up on television, showing Derby County beaten 4-1 by Shrewsbury Town at Gay Meadow. It sounded a good one to miss but that was only a temporary thought as a classic struggle developed, almost exhausting to watch as the advantage swayed and tension was maintained. The first phase belonged to Northamptonshire as Geoff Cook and Wayne Larkins, Ned to everybody in cricket, set off with a partnership of 99 in 29 overs. The September dew, often a decisive factor in Gillette Finals, was apparently banished by the new sponsors because the pitch was bland and neither opener was in the slightest trouble. Colin Tunnicliffe was, conceding 23 from his first three overs, but Geoff Miller began a fruitful day by dismissing Larkins with a fine running catch on the mid-wicket boundary. Soon afterwards, he struck an even more crucial blow by running out the dangerous Allan Lamb with a direct hit. It was a tight decision and television cameras were not then sited square of the stumps to show line decisions but some time later, I was shown a photograph taken by a Derbyshire supporter, Andrew Kennedy, which showed

Lamb was in before the wicket was broken. It was a major stroke of luck for Derbyshire. Miller was still occupying the centre of the stage when he joined the attack and, thanks to a spectacular flying catch by Alan Hill, dismissed Richard Williams. Cook completed a chanceless century but the early momentum was never regained and Northamptonshire closed at 235 for nine. Derbyshire felt they had done well to restrict them and made an equally good start. Hill contributed to an opening stand of 41 but the vital partnership, 123, was shared by the two overseas players, John Wright and Peter Kirsten. They appeared in the mood to win it themselves but were out in the same over from Neil Mallender as 164 for one became 165 for three. Runs now had to be chiselled and the most important stroke of the day was Miller's pull for six off Sarfraz Nawaz. The Pakistan Test player was vulnerable in the closing stages because, while Jim Griffiths was mean at one end, Miller and Tunnicliffe found it comparatively safe to attack Sarfraz. Derbyshire, well aware of the playing conditions from the semi-final, needed six from Griffiths' final over, one from the last ball of the day, to draw level. Cook spent an age making sure the field was right but Tunnicliffe got something on it, pad or edge against pad, and Miller, ready for the sprint, dived over the line before Cook ran in to take off the bails. The scores were tied but Derbyshire had lost only six wickets. I wanted to sit back and let it all wash over me but there was work to be done, dressing-room reaction to be recorded. It was the joy on Tunnicliffe's face as he came in with his medal that cracked me up. He emerged from local cricket for a debut in 1973 but found it hard to take wickets with his left-arm seam and was released the following year. After two summers with Langley Mill, he returned for a second, more successful try but taking five wickets in an innings was an insurmountable barrier until he achieved it at Northampton in June, 1980. Having proved to himself that it was possible, he repeated it in each of the four competitions in 1981. By the NatWest Final, he was 32 and this might be his one chance of glory. His day began badly but after his costly first three overs, the other nine cost only a further 19, with two wickets. He was not only back in the game but his mood was right for an innings at the decisive time. Tunnicliffe came in from the balcony with his medal and the expression of a man who could hardly credit what had happened to him. It has to be confessed that I shed a few tears of embarrassing pleasure on his behalf.

There is nowhere quite like winning dressing-rooms and, on all but big occasions, they remain private, but even at the moment of Derbyshire's first success since the 1936 Championship, there was a worrying under-current. Opinions were needed from Wright and Kirsten, whose partner-ship took Derbyshire along the right road, but both seemed to need confir-mation that they made a contribution. Wood, it later emerged, said some-thing in the heat of the moment and it was not long before the winning team began to break up. Mike Hendrick, who battled through his 12 overs despite carrying a groin strain, and Miller wanted to leave because of, as it was put, general dissatisfaction with Derbyshire, while Steele, nearing 40, was rejoining Northamptonshire. Wood was dismissive: "Hendo and Mills have made their own decisions," he said. "If they are not happy with the club, they will be unable to give of their best." Hendrick moved to Nottinghamshire but Miller changed his mind and stayed. The lasting memorial to Derbyshire's great day was the building of the pavilion during 1981-82, at last giving the County Ground something to identify it as a first-class venue. The project owed much to the driving enthusiasm of two committee members, Tony Blount and Roy Osbourne, but they, like the new chief executive Roger Pearman, were, in the end, poorly treated by the county. Far from setting off a successful era, the NatWest Trophy was an end in itself, immediately followed by a period of strife. Wood led the team exceptionally well after he took over from Miller in mid-season, not miss-ing a trick on the way to holding up the Trophy, but as appointed captain for 1982, the flaws began to show. Peter Hacker, for example, came from Nottinghamshire to bolster the seam department when Hendrick went in the opposite direction and was away to a good start, 21 wickets in his first five Championship matches. The left-arm bowler was nippy and, although erratic, capable of surprising batsmen but after injuring a shoulder in early June, was hardly given another game. While moaning about weaknesses in the attack, Wood appeared to have decided Hacker was not much of a bowler and Tunnicliffe also found himself on the outside for no good reason. Kirsten, who scored eight centuries in 1982, was also disenchanted and, it was suggested, fancied the captaincy. When he announced he was taking 1983 off to explore business opportunities in South Africa, it was generally accepted that he would not return to Derbyshire. Wood blocked the appointment of Philip Russell as cricket manager and when they played at Scarborough in September, asked the players to affirm their confidence in him but, although a secret ballot went against him, he was reappointed for 1983. The committee did it in such a way that they had the worst of both worlds, a captain regarded with suspicion by his men and Wood upset because he had only a one-year deal as a player. He delayed before accepting then, in the second Championship match, at Grace Road, Leicester, suddenly resigned, claiming that the responsibility was making it impossible for him to maintain his standards as a player. In a sopping wet spring, Derbyshire had played on only two days, so his case totally failed to stand up, looking more like a challenge to the committee. If so, it did not work and, after Miller briefly held the fort, Derbyshire took a bold decision by elevating Kim Barnett to the captaincy at the age of 22. Wood never again played in the Championship and when he was omitted from the one-day side, declared himself: "Flabbergasted and insulted." In cricket terms, it was fair comment: he had, after all, regained a place in England's one-day side in 1982 but he was making waves. His contract was cancelled in July and it was a sad way to end a fine career. The trouble was he was not content to confine himself to the duties of captaincy. He wanted a say in everything, so fell out with committee members and administrative staff as well as players. After the magical day at Lord's he could, had he played it right, been with Derbyshire for years, as coach or cricket manager when he retired, because he knew the game. Unfortunately, he was less good at people.

Mike Hendrick, who left at the age of 32, was a bowler in Derbyshire's best tradition, accurate and niggardly, quick enough to make batsmen wary, expert in using the seam. He was not an out-and-out fast bowler – few of the Derbyshire greats have been – nor did he swing the ball. Although Hendrick grew up in Darlington and Leicestershire, he was born in Darley Dale and home produced as a county player. He almost did not make it because of early problems with sore shins but, fortunately, was given another year and began to blossom in 1972. He went on to play in 30 Tests, his economy often proving an effective foil to Ian Botham's more adventurous seam bowling at the other end. He once came home from a Test in some confusion, having been told he should pitch the ball further up. Hendrick knew that if he bowled a fuller length at his pace, batsmen would be only too happy to attack him and this desire to change people is one of the things that has always baffled me about selectors. The way Hendrick bowled for Derbyshire earned him a Test place: that was the bowler he was. If they wanted a different style, they should have looked elsewhere but Hendrick clearly merited inclusion on his own terms. In his years as captain in the 1950s, Guy Willatt rejected similar pressure from the chairman of cricket, Guy Jackson, over the great Les Jackson. Guy Jackson was a fine captain himself, rebuilding a team between 1922 and 1930, but always wanted Les to pitch the ball further up. "How can he bowl without a mid-off?" was the question. He didn't need one was the answer and a generation of batsmen would have been profoundly grateful had Les amended his style. The most absurd example was in South Africa in 1995-96 when the manager, Ray Illingworth, and his coach, Peter Lever, tried to turn Devon Malcolm, then past 30, into a line-and-length bowler. Sheer pace earned Malcolm an England career and enabled him to blitz the South Africans at the Oval in 1994. There was no secret about what Malcolm brought to the table and an attempt to retrain him at that stage of his life was so stupid as to be beyond belief. Miller was a player who always looked the part from the moment he made his debut. He was born and educated in Chesterfield before he slipped smoothly into Derbyshire cricket. In one of his early one-day matches, he was fielding in the covers and did a dummy run at the path of a stroke. He may have been able to reach the ball with a desperate dive but there was no suggestion that was on the agenda. It was real 'old soldier' fielding and had the effect of galvanising a reluctant Fred Rumsey into a long and fruitless chase to the boundary. Miller, obviously at home on a cricket field, always threatened more than he achieved. He was a good all-rounder but the potential appeared to be there for something more dominant. I say appeared because, over a long career, status is proved by returns and there is no point in disputing the figures. Miller is an easy-going personality and trying to assume a harder shell when he was appointed captain proved impossible. He played in 34 Tests but was never allowed the luxury of feeling he was an established member of the team. Penetrating the inner circle at Test level is hard and there are many tales of players who would have settled for a welcome to the club instead of being treated as interlopers. Kim Barnett springs to mind, along with Mike Smith, a talented Gloucestershire seamer, and two from Northamptonshire, Paul Taylor and David Capel. Taylor began his career with Derbyshire but was released in 1986 and went into the Minor Counties with Staffordshire. It was sad, because he was an electric fielder and left-arm fast bowlers give an invaluable variation but his success with Northamptonshire showed the nice guys sometimes prevail. The great saga with Miller was the wait for his maiden century. It was always within his grasp but there were some disasters along the way. At Derby, he was once cruelly run out by David Steele, one to preserve his wicket at all costs even if it meant diving to reach the line before his partner. He was going well at Bath on another occasion but, immediately before the tea interval, tried to pull a half-volley and inevitably suffered. David Baggett, editor of Derbyshire's invaluable *Year Book*, produced a wonderfully abstruse statistic in the 2003 edition to demonstrate that Miller held a world record for the most half-centuries, 56 in all first-class games, before he finally reached the maiden hundred against Lancashire at Old Trafford in 1984.

Hendrick and Miller evolved a splendid double act which, when the mood was right, convulsed bars and hotel lounges around the world. They assumed the parts of Sam and Arthur, two old codgers from north Derbyshire sitting in a pub discussing the cricket from a basis of scant knowledge and with a facility for getting the names wrong. So Derbyshire's legendary opening bowlers became Jackman and Gladstone, while there was much discussion of a more contemporary captain, Eric Baslow. This usually concluded with the triumphant assertion: "E's an African, tha knos". When they took this with them on England tours, a few props were added, mufflers and a couple of old cloth caps. Bob Taylor was their companion in Tests, often giving Derbyshire three in the same England side. For years, Taylor had to be content with one appearance, in New Zealand at the end of the 1969-70 tour, and believed that would be his lot, in common with the immaculate Northamptonshire wicketkeeper Keith Andrew, one of his role models. Alan Knott held sway and while there was little to choose between their talents behind the stumps, the Kent man generally offered more runs. Knott had eccentric dietary habits, especially for survival through India and Pakistan, and some of the studied scruffiness typical of a later master of the art, Jack Russell of Gloucestershire. Taylor was 36 when his second chance came as a result of Knott joining Kerry Packer's World Series and so removing himself from contention. It was time enough for Taylor to build a considerable England career, although the selectors made an error by picking Paul Downton ahead of him for the first Test against Australia in 1981. Downton spilled an important catch and that series turned into fantasy when Ian Botham surrendered the captaincy to Mike Brearley. Botham immediately recovered his wonderful touch as a player and the Headingley Test, which England won after following on, almost brought the country to a halt. Derbyshire were at Taunton while the drama developed and Eric Hill, the delightful resident journalist, brought his radio into the Press box. Hill, a former Somerset player, always preserved the courtesies and would not normally have countenanced such an intrusion but, on this occasion, it was impossible to avoid being swept along by events at Leeds. From there, the Derbyshire caravan moved to Worcester and, when Taylor arrived to join them, he was still so excited that it was almost impossible to interview him. Wisely, we agreed to have another shot the following morning, before leaving for New Road. No player could hope for a better summer than Taylor enjoyed in 1981 but there was no overt triumphalism, more a gracious acceptance.

Steve Oldham was 12th man when Derbyshire won at Lord's but, in his four seasons following a move from Yorkshire, demonstrated how a good professional went about his business. He knew his capabilities and, therefore, his limitations. "At my pace, I'll be smashed if I don't put the ball in the right place," he said of his medium-paced seam bowling. There were good days and he was proud to be capped in 1980, his first season. Leaner times never came through lack of effort. When I wrote in a *Year Book* farewell that he could always enjoy his evening pint with a clear conscience, Esso, as he was universally known because of his initials, made a point of thanking me for the observation. He returned to Yorkshire as a coach and played a considerable, if often unheralded, part in developing a succession of good young players. For years after my embarrassing moment in the Lord's dressing-room, he was liable to remark: "I can put up with owt provided Ged doesn't burst into tears again."

HIGH COURT
REPORTER

I N August 1984, Ian Maxwell became the eighth Derby County chairman in less than eight years. They went through managers at almost the same rate as the decline, on and off the field, accelerated. From being League champions in 1975, Derby launched their Centenary season, 1984-85, in the Third Division having given another classic display of misrule. While relegation from the First Division in 1980 did not involve a plunge into the financial abyss that awaits those losing a Premiership place in the modern game, the crisis at the time was severe enough and ultimately took Derby into the High Court. As chairmen changed and new directors joined the board, various financial initiatives were launched as rescue plans. Well meant they may have been but all they did was buy time, increasingly little, and ward off the evil day of reckoning. Derby boards would be the worst Snakes and Ladders players in the world because they always manage to land on the giant snake, the one that takes you back to the start. Supporters feel helpless as debts rise because, with the best will in the world, they do not flock to see a bad team and the money involved is beyond their compass. In the early 1980s, a £1.5m deficit was alarming enough, especially when the Inland Revenue and VAT inspectors became alarmed that their demands were ignored. That looked negligible in the early years of the new millennium, when the debt was £30m and rising: and still the Rams were trying to buy time. If a manager is to be effective, he must have a measure of stability coming from those over him, not bickering incompetence.

Waiting to see who occupied the chairman's seat at the 1979 team photograph was enough to tell Colin Addison and John Newman that the omens were not good although the new man in the middle, Richard Moore, allowed them to spend money that the club could not afford. Barry Powell, at £350,000 from Coventry City, was not a success. Although he had great stamina, he was not a player to take the lead in midfield, more one to fit into an established pattern. Unfortunately for him, there was no solid base and, in the first half of the season, Derby were desperately short of goals. A startling FA Cup defeat, 6-2 by Bristol City at Ashton Gate, convinced Addison of the need for action, especially as City were also struggling members of the First Division. The episode revealed alarming cracks in the club as David Langan, the excellent Republic of Ireland defender developed under Colin Murphy, refused to travel to the game. He was ordered to make his own way but, in the argument that developed when he arrived, Langan was supported by Bruce Rioch and both were sent home. Langan was soon back in the side, peace having been made, but Rioch's second spell with Derby was a messy affair, especially for one who set sound disciplinary standards when he went into management. With such evidence of disruption, a positive step was necessary and Addison provided it with the £350,000 signing of Alan Biley, a bright young striker from Cambridge United. Biley, with his hair styled in the manner of Rod Stewart, had the personality to lift a side, provided all was well in his own department. The following month, David Swindlehurst arrived from Crystal Palace, initially on loan, and their partnership promised much. Michael Dunford, the secretary, likened the tall, strong Swindlehurst to forwards emerging at that time from the Soviet Union and in April 1980, a permanent deal secured him for £400,000. Along with Keith Osgood, another from Coventry, and temporary deals for Trevor Whymark and Roger Davies, the expenditure was considerable but Derby still went down. Optimism based around Biley and Swindlehurst led to chants of 'We'll be back in '81' but Derby were in poorer shape than most fans realised. Although Langan resumed his place after the spat at Bristol, he joined Birmingham City for

£350,000 in the summer and formed a fruitful liaison with Jim Smith that continued into Oxford United's remarkable rise from Third Division to First in successive seasons after Robert Maxwell invested in the club just outside his back garden at Headington Hill Hall. By the time Oxford won the League Cup in 1986, Smith had left, increasingly exasperated by trying to deal with Maxwell. Ironically, he was managing Queen's Park Rangers, Oxford's opponents at Wembley. "As we lined up in the tunnel, I looked at the players and realised I knew the Oxford team far better than my own," Smith told me when he became Derby's manager. Oxford, inspired by Trevor Hebberd, were much the better side and, when the game ended, I looked round the pitch for Langan. He was shattered, thinning hair plastered to his skull, shorts in danger of slipping off, socks round his ankles. Smith and Oxford prolonged his career: once, after victory over Birmingham, the club that rejected both, player and manager made deep inroads into a bottle of Scotch on the coach home, marking the strength of their feeling about people at St Andrew's. Langan also suffered injuries that severely hampered him after he gave up the game but he was one of the best players to emerge from Derby's Youth team. Derby needed the money from his sale but landed in Division Two with an alarming thud, beaten 3-0 by Cambridge at the Abbey Stadium on the opening day.

Davies was playing in the North American Soccer League when Addison brought him back for 23 games, as one of Derby's greats had been doing. When Tommy Docherty squeezed him out in an insulting way, Kevin Hector joined Vancouver Whitecaps. Alan Hinton was assistant coach as well as a player, setting all sorts of NASL records for 'assists', and the move worked well. In the NASL off-seasons, Hector played on loan for Boston United and Burton Albion, so was able to maintain his home in Derby. Albion thought they had him on a permanent basis but, in October 1980, Addison brought him back to the Baseball Ground. Hector was 35 and the days when his pace could worry top English defence had gone. But he kept his enthusiasm as well as his fitness, was a fine player and helped Derby for two seasons. To supporters, he remained King Kevin but Addison's move was not a populist gesture: the simple fact was that Hector improved the squad. By the time he left, Hector held the appearance records for Derby in the League and all matches, while his 201 goals put him behind only Steve Bloomer. Biley was enduring a disappointing second season and, in February, was on the point of joining West Bromwich Albion, with David Mills moving in the opposite direction. An ankle injury scuppered the deal and when Biley went to Everton the following summer, Addison knew that none of the £300,000 fee was available for strengthening the team. In 1980-81, Derby finished sixth and, while that was a respectable return, it was clear that they were not advancing. Roy McFarland's great Derby career ended in summer when he joined Bradford City as player-manager and I remember sitting in the office with Newman after the decision was made. We attacked the Scotch as willingly as Smith and Langan had done before Newman remembered that he was due to present the Cup for the local final in progress outside. In the Fourth Division, McFarland's class stood out and he promptly led them to promotion. David Markham, who was the *Telegraph and Argus* man at Valley Parade, kept in touch and said once: "Roy was able to dominate games, through his presence as well as his skill. So often, he was easily the best man on the field and we found it hard to take our eyes off him." Stuart Webb's ordeal, which began when police were called to the Baseball Ground, ended in October 1980, when it was decided there was no case to answer. The investigation was both long and extremely expensive as it involved detectives visiting the United States to transfers between Derby and NASL clubs. Webb was relieved: "There were times when I wondered if I had two heads, as so many people stared and pointed in the street." He was also bitter about the way he was dumped by Derby's directors but, although he bided his time, his involvement with the club was by no means over.

Financial worries, which had obviously developed, became a more public issue in 1981-82, starting with a hint that Doug Ellis might be interested in taking over. At the time, Ellis was off the Aston Villa board and told associates that his 'football money' was lying idle. Nothing came of it and he later returned for a long innings as Villa chairman. As he doubled as chief executive, successful Villa managers found his constant presence wearing but, in his defence, it has to be said that Ellis always kept the club solvent, even while Villa Park was being developed. With Derby's overdraft running past £1-million, Richard Moore announced a survival plan but it did not carry him anywhere as, in the same month, he resigned as chairman. He was succeeded by Bill Stevenson, a heating and ventilation engineer who could never escape the tag given him by Neil Hallam in the *Derby Trader*, the Belper Plumber. The *Trader*, a free sheet owned, built up and run by Lionel Pickering, always offered a salty view of the club's affairs. Later, when Pickering bought Derby County, he saw Hallam's column from a different angle and the writer was banned from Press areas, an unreasonable prohibition that was maintained for years. When Stevenson took the chair, John Kirkland at last joined the board, instead of sitting outside it with the large slab of shares gathered by his father Jack. It was a healthier situation but all was not well on the field and a crowd of 8,470 for a midweek match against Cambridge indicated the level of disenchantment around the Baseball Ground. The FA Cup brought no relief and saw the end of Mick Coop as a Derby player. He served Coventry well in more than 400 League games and arrived on a free transfer in the hope that his experience would be valuable. He had a bad time and it came to a head when he was run ragged by Jeff Chandler as Bolton Wanderers won 3-1. On a vile day, Derby supporters were drenched in an uncovered part of Burnden Park and found it hard to forgive Coop, who went off with barely a speck of mud on him. It was soon the end for Addison, who described himself as 'Sad, disappointed, relieved,' when he was dismissed. He was unable to achieve the success he craved for Derby but the relief came with the realisation that he was banging his head against the wall. His enthusiasm for the game never dimmed and he always found employment. One of the features of 2002-03 was the way he revived Forest Green Rovers in the Nationwide Conference. Newman agreed to take over but, having seen the state of the club from inside, knew exactly how difficult it would be. Derby approved the issue of 600,000 £1 shares, with a £9 premium, ten of which I bought as a gesture. They did not sell enough to make a significant impact and Derby were not completely safe from relegation until Hector bowed out with the winner in the final game, at home to Watford. Charlie George, another reminder of prosperous days, helped but could not agree on terms to prolong his stay into the following season. As Newman said: "The atmosphere round the place was so flat that we desperately needed somebody to give us a lift. Charlie did that. He was fine but it was a battle on all fronts." After Derby had come close to ending the struggle with a point from a dim game at Oldham, I spoke to Charlie in the hope of a cheering message. Instead, he was totally realistic, punctuated by some expertly aimed spits into a corner, and concluded that nothing would improve the following season because there were not enough good players at the club. The most obvious sign of crisis is an inability to pay the wages on time and they were late in October 1983. In one of the strangest chapters in the Derby County story, they were paid by Anton Johnson, chairman of Rotherham United, and delivered by his commercial manager John Adams, whose son Chris later played cricket for Derbyshire, Sussex and England. There was talk of a consortium involving Johnson and one of his associates, Alistair Ward, a prospect that Derby people found alarming. Johnson, with his fur coat and night clubs in Essex, was the kind of chairman who provoked quizzical looks from football's establishment and, of course, there was a League rule prohibiting a major stake in more than one club. Instead, it was Mike Watterson, based in Chesterfield, who took over. Watterson had seen the potential impact of snooker when shown on colour television and was extremely successful in raising the game's profile. Snooker's subsequent popularity, especially with the use of the Crucible Theatre in Sheffield as a venue for the World Championship, owes much to his drive and vision. He brought in Webb as a director, sacked Newman as manager and persuaded Peter Taylor to return to Derby. This infuriated Brian Clough, who was under the impression that his former partner was retiring from the game for good when he left Nottingham Forest. After Watterson's arrival, Newman was left dangling as he waited for a week to be told the fate he knew was inevitable. In different circumstances, Newman would have been as effective at Derby as he was with Exeter City and Grimsby Town but he was well aware what he was taking on when Addison left. In one of Newman's early games in charge, Derby were hammered 6-1 by Watford at Vicarage Road and Graham Taylor, with sympathy for a fellow manager, emphasised in his

Press conference that clubs where directors were always in the news had no chance.

Taylor brought back one of Derby's Champions, Archie Gemmill, who was with Wigan Athletic on a non-contract basis after an NASL summer with Jacksonville Tea Men, and made moves to restore another, Roy McFarland, as his assistant. Bradford City did not accept that without a fight and when Derby went to discuss a possible solution, there were allegations of a bugged boardroom at Valley Parade. When McFarland resigned to join Derby, Bradford chairman Bob Martin complained to the Football League about poaching. After a hearing at Lytham St Annes, Derby were fined and ordered to pay compensation but, if all the evidence had been more fully investigated, the case was not as one-sided as it sounded. McFarland was accompanied to Derby by his number two Mick Jones, once on Derby's books and later a player with Notts County. Ken Gutteridge was added to the staff as Alan Ashman, Richie Norman and Ron Webster lost their jobs. There was particular sympathy for Webster, who played in the two Championship teams and was an effective Youth coach who had a good touch with those under his command. Derby were even able to find some money, £80,000 for Halifax Town's 23-year-old forward Bobby Davison, who had given the Rams a fright in the League Cup earlier that season. Davison, with his bright, alert eyes, was a natural scorer and, in time, became one of only 10 to pass 100 goals for Derby. His eager attitude soon endeared him to supporters and, on the playing side, he became the one significant legacy of Taylor's time as manager. The FA Cup offered a chance to lift the public further, giving Derby a home draw against Nottingham Forest in the third round. With Clough and Taylor publicly at odds, it was certain to be a fraught occasion, much as the two managers tried to play down its significance. It turned out to be a bad day for Forest, beaten by goals from Gemmill and Andy Hill, a young striker signed by Addison from Kimberley Town. As the Baseball Ground corridors throbbed afterwards, Taylor criticised the reaction. "It shows everything that's wrong with this club," he grumbled but there had been precious little to celebrate for too many years. The great Clough and Taylor principle was that the League provided the bread and butter. Taylor was trying to make that point and still faced a battle to survive in Division Two but he put it over in an eccentric fashion. Derby also eliminated Chelsea, through two goals from Kevin Wilson, before losing to Manchester United but the Cup brought people back through the turnstiles and Taylor was able to do some trading. Paul Futcher, an elegant if moody central defender, was signed from Oldham Athletic and John Richards, out of the Wolverhampton Wanderers side, volunteered to join on loan. Taylor appealed for experienced players to help and Richards, an intelligent striker, answered the call for 10 games. At the end of January, Derby set out on a remarkable run of 15 games without defeat. As nine of them were drawn, Derby inched rather than soared towards safety but the club record of 22 was not far out of sight and sequences like that normally belong to good sides, not clubs in turmoil. Swindlehurst left for West Ham United in March, enabling Taylor to bring in Paul Hooks from Notts County and another trusted ally, defender Kenny Burns on loan from Leeds United. Burns, who had formed a fine defensive partnership with Larry Lloyd, was an integral part of Forest's greatest team, elected Footballer of the Year when he was at the City Ground: "I trust Kenny," said Taylor. The good work was endangered in May when, in successive away trips, Derby were comprehensively beaten by Blackburn Rovers and Crystal Palace, so they had to win their final home game, against a Fulham side chasing promotion, to be absolutely safe. Davison's stunning goal earned them victory and, as it turned out, Derby already had enough points. More importantly, the game ended in chaos as fans were allowed through the barriers and ringed two sides of the pitch. One tripped Robert Wilson, an insane act, but hundreds were close enough to have done something similar. Ray Chadwick, in his last game as a League referee, added almost four minutes of stoppage-time before abandoning the match with, he said, 78 seconds remaining. He should have stopped it earlier and insisted that spectators returned to their proper places but, having accepted the clearly unsatisfactory situation, was silly to prolong the action for so long. It was hard for the referee and heaven only knew what the police were doing in allowing barriers to be opened. Malcolm Macdonald, then Fulham's manager, wanted the game to be played again and seemed to have a fair case. "Are you a betting man, Malcolm?" asked Taylor. "I'm telling you now there'll be no replay." It had been a bad season for crowd trouble, with frightening scenes at the Baseball Ground when Leeds and Chelsea were the visitors. Taylor was ridiculed in newspapers when he suggested snatch squads to bring out the ringleaders but nobody offered a more practical solution, only hand-wringing from the League, the FA and clubs. When Watterson resigned as chairman in July, leaving as suddenly as he came, he gave crowd violence as one of his contributory reasons, although another may well have been the intimate knowledge he acquired about the financial perils ahead.

As if relations with Clough were not already bad enough, Taylor signed John Robertson, who was out of contract at the City Ground, on a free transfer. Ever since he was weighing up Forest's players, on a 1976 pre-season tour after leaving Brighton to resume his partnership with Clough, Taylor had been obsessed by Robertson's quality. Taylor was a good enough judge to see past first impressions, which were of a scruffy, over-weight Scottish winger who was in danger of wasting his career. Taylor accused him of living out of a chip pan which, in typical fashion, became one of his running jokes for the next decade. The potential Taylor saw lay in Robertson's ability to hold the ball, bring defenders towards him and use it to good effect. Once he discovered somebody had faith in him, Robertson became one of the most influential wide players in Europe, although there was no noticeable improvement in his dress sense. Forest favoured the pass to Robertson on the left, just as Derby used Alan Hinton so effectively. They won the Championship that way and when I went to Munich to see the European Cup Final against Malmo in 1979, I was already rising from my seat when Robertson found that vital yard of space and shaped to cross. He aimed it perfectly and Trevor Francis, England's first £1m player, headed in the only goal of the game. A year later, when Forest successfully defended the trophy, Robertson scored the one goal needed to beat Hamburg. He could play but Taylor's error lay in seeing him as the jewel in Derby's crown. For all the optimism engendered by the previous season's long, unbeaten run and successful escape from relega-tion, there was no crown, hardly a cloth cap. Robertson needed to be playing in a good side and Derby were again struggling for their lives. Taylor admitted his mistake and, on reflection, wished he had signed a couple of craggy defenders rather than Robertson and Bobby Campbell, a centre-forward from Bradford City who suffered a nightmare and was back at Valley Parade, on loan and then, inevitably at a loss, in November. The crowd gave up on him in a home defeat by Grimsby Town at the end of October, a day remarkable for an extraordinary misjudgement. Taylor, McFarland and Jones were away looking for new players, so Ken Gutteridge was left in charge of the team. As the season had been going horribly wrong since the first, opening-day whistle blew on a 5-0 defeat by Chelsea at Stamford Bridge, there was an obvious need for reinforcement but not at the expense of the entire management team being elsewhere. Chelsea had one of those days when every shot zoomed into the top corner but further humiliations followed quickly. Simon Garner scored all Blackburn's goals in a 5-1 defeat at Ewood Park and Malcolm Poskett almost emulated him when Carlisle won 4-1 at the Baseball Ground. Kirkland, reluctantly, succeeded Watterson as chairman and found he was facing similar problems to those which finished his predecessors. The October wages were a fortnight late and an attempt to engage County Council support as guarantors failed. The board consulted a liquidation expert and sat uneasily when he told them they were effectively trading illegally. The Inland Revenue pounced first when, in February 1984, they issued a winding-up petition in pursuit of unpaid taxes. They were soon joined by Customs and Excise, chasing VAT arrears, and the severity of the problem was now clear for all to see. Derby were not merely in trouble but in danger of disappearing. The NatWest Bank froze the account, so they could neither pay in nor withdraw cash, no help to Telford United, who were keen to lay their hands on the share of the receipts from a fourth round FA Cup tie, watched by 21,488, at the Baseball Ground. It was one of those times when football writers attempt to pass themselves off as financial experts while management and players try to continue as if nothing was wrong.

By then, Stuart Webb was in dogged pursuit of financial assistance. First, with the active backing of chairman John Kirkland, he set about acquiring enough shares to gain control of the club. "It struck me at the time that Derby County needed to be speaking with one voice if we were to make any progress," Webb said later. "The situation was extremely serious and I do not think we would have completed the season had action not been taken then." It was clearly best that the one voice should belong to Webb as, not for the last time, he was the only board member known in football. There were, as usual, a few people around Derby who promised to put in money but never sat down to write a cheque. It was obvious that outside investment was required and there were rumours, ultimately coming to nothing, of a consortium based in Hong Kong. By February 1984, it was clear that Robert Maxwell was the target. Maxwell had already discovered that football suited him because, although head of a considerable publishing business and a former Labour MP, he gained far more recognition when galumphing round the Manor Ground as chairman of a successful Oxford United. Publicity appealed to him for its own sake, as there was a massive ego to be nurtured, and he was aware it could be exploited to his financial advantage. He alienated Oxford supporters by proposing to merge them with Reading into a hybrid called Thames Valley Royals, then fought a running battle with the Council over the cramped facilities at their headquarters in Headington. As Oxford knew, he had more financial clout than anybody else likely to become involved with the club and was looking for a bigger stage. He wanted to take over Manchester United but cribbed at the asking price of £15m which, in retrospect, was not one of his better business decisions. It was hard to pin him down and Webb spent countless hours on trains, heading for meetings that sometimes left him in despair. He often called me late at night, both to keep his local paper in touch but also to use me as a sounding board and seek encouragement. At the beginning of March, Derby called a Press conference to announce that Maxwell had agreed in principle to join in organising 'a financial reconstruction and rescue of the club'. Once the High Court approved the plan he would, it was said, sever all connections with Oxford United to become Derby's chairman. If that sounded simple, Webb soon discovered he was on an obstacle course, his meetings taking on an air of crisis. For a start, the Revenue blocked all suggestions of a cut-price deal with Maxwell. They did not regard themselves as unsecured creditors but wanted their money in full: even 70p in the pound was of no interest to them. As Derby's appearances in the High Court began, there was a constant background threat that Maxwell would pull away and leave them in an unsustainable position. For the first hearing, David Moore (*The Mirror*), Roger Duckworth (*The Sun*) and I travelled on the early train from Derby with Webb. Only when we arrived did it become clear that Derby's case would not be heard until the afternoon but I sat in court for an hour, observing businesses being wound-up at an alarming rate. Some owners made their own pleas in order to save money on fees but, if they won a temporary reprieve, were strongly advised by the judge to have legal representation next time they appeared. No Trade Union could have been more efficient at ensuring any money was kept in house. Nor did Court reporters, with their ordered existence and immaculate shorthand, take kindly to the Socceroos clambering round them in the small Press area.

While Derby made seven High Court appearances, there was still a football season in progress and they floundered horribly in the Second Division, winning only once between mid-December and the beginning of April, but had a chance of being the most unlikely FA Cup Finalists of modern times. They began by beating Cambridge United at the Abbey Stadium, then eliminated Telford thanks to Davison's hat-trick. The fifth round victory over Norwich City at the Baseball Ground was more convincing than 2-1 suggests, Chris Woods doing much to limit the score, although he was lucky to stay on after racing out of his area to flatten Kevin Wilson. In the sixth round, Derby were drawn to face Plymouth Argyle, down in the lower end of the Third Division, at Home Park. Plymouth always appear to have potential to be a big club but it never happens, largely because they are out on a limb. They had no trouble filling the ground with 34,365 for this tie and should have won. Derby survived a battering thanks to three players, Steve Cherry in goal and the two central defenders, Paul Futcher and Kenny Burns. Poor Cherry, whose decisive act was to touch Gordon Staniforth's late shot against one post, from where it rolled along the line to hit the other, was beaten in the replay when a corner by Alan Rogers went straight in. He never lived that down in Derby but it was a cruel judgement because there would have been no replay without his heroic efforts in the first game. As the winners faced Watford, Derby fancied their chances but blew it and, on the same day, another proposal was rejected in the High Court. Maxwell threatened to walk away but the Football League had a clear stance on such situations, that tax and VAT debts must be paid in full. "Mr Maxwell knew it before he became involved," said League secretary Graham Kelly. Webb always regarded this as his darkest hour as his plan seemed to be in ruins and he did not know the replay result until he alighted at Nottingham station. Maxwell had a valid position, that it was irresponsible of the Revenue and Custom and Excise to allow debts to escalate out of control, but he also knew that he could not bully them into a deal. There was further alarm when Derby City Council added weight to the winding-up petitions but Maxwell's tactics were designed to push directors into coming up with more money themselves. Futcher and Calvin Plummer moved to Barnsley for a combined fee of £40,000 but Derby still took on another wage by signing Burns on a free transfer from Leeds after his second loan expired. By the time he left, Futcher despaired of Taylor, whose relations with several players had collapsed. It is one thing to make harsh judgements from a position of strength, when replacements can be secured, but Taylor wrote off players he was soon forced to pick again. Futcher and Plummer made their Barnsley debuts against Derby in a 5-1 rout, compounded when Burns was sent off. At Oakwell, unusually, progress from the field to the dressing-rooms is up a slope and Taylor, his face drained of colour after the final whistle, gave a grimace of utter despair that I shall never forget. He had failed, for the first time in his career, and knew the game was up, that there was no way back for him. Two days later, Webb was in the High Court for the last time and, in a fine display of brinkmanship, the relevant money was delivered to him in the well-appointed gentleman's lavatory. Mr Justice Mervyn Davies, who sat for all Derby's seven appearances, wrapped it up in seven words. "Very well. Lift the petition. No costs." There was a modest celebration in the Wig and Pen, on the other side of the Strand, and Webb returned home to succeed Kirkland as chairman.

His first act was to end Taylor's contract 'by mutual consent', a formula that allowed a dignified departure. Only 11 months earlier, Taylor was a hero and although he made plenty of mistakes, managing a sick club is an unforgiving task. Roy McFarland was given temporary charge, nine games in search of a miracle, and began with a 3-0 victory over Crystal Palace, remarkable for Andy Garner's hat-trick at the age of 18. They did enough to cling on until the final fortnight but hope effectively disappeared when they were poor relations at Newcastle United's celebration party. The return of Kevin Keegan to English football inspired Newcastle and their manager, Arthur Cox, provided him with others on the same wavelength, Peter Beardsley, Terry McDermott, Chris Waddle, Glenn Roeder. It was an entertaining team on the brink of the First Division and they pulverised the Rams with a 4-0 exhibition. For people from Derby, it was time to slide away and let the Geordies enjoy themselves. The Rams were down two days later when Oldham beat Grimsby to put themselves beyond reach. Champions to Division Three, for the Centenary season, in nine years but at least there was a club and soon there was a manager.

Just three weeks after his Newcastle side trampled all over the Rams, Arthur Cox was installed at the Baseball Ground. He was unimpressed by the way Newcastle dallied and dithered over a new contract and resigned on a matter of principle. Considering the level of football Cox supervised at St James' Park, where he proved an ability to handle experienced play-ers as well as nurturing emerging talents such as Beadsley, Waddle and Paul Gascoigne, his appointment was a remarkable coup for a club so recently relegated. He was known in the area, having managed Chesterfield for four years, narrowly missing promotion and, remarkably, being the biggest spender one transfer deadline day. That was a change from the days when Arthur Sutherland, the long-serving secretary, guarded the coffers and classified agreements for players under only three categories, free, nominal and substantial, the last not nudging £10,000 too hard. Considering Cox's record, there was surprisingly little overt enthu-siasm for the appointment but several factors could have influenced that. The whole season, including the desperate search for backers, left supporters sandbagged and the vast majority remembered when the Rams had a reputation in Europe. Now they contemplated Division Three with a slender playing staff that did not promise an immediate return. Many, too, hoped that Roy McFarland would have the job although, in all honesty, it demanded greater management experience than he had at the time. So Cox arrived at a glum club but one of the first things he did was to ask McFarland to act as his assistant. Then he set about engaging players and an early signing turned out to be one of the best imaginable. Because of a technicality on the offer of a new contract, Rob Hindmarch was available on a free transfer from Sunderland and Cox nipped in, saying: "I would have signed Rob if I had still been manager of Newcastle." Hindmarch was Sunderland's captain when still a teenager and was a natural leader. He was 23 when he joined Derby and although he was not immediately appointed captain, it was inevitable that he would assume the office sooner rather than later. Hindmarch had no pace but was a massive figure in the centre of defence, fearless, totally committed, ready to battle against all odds. He gave Derby mental as well as physical strength and there was great sadness in the city when, in 2002, he died in Philadelphia of motor neurone disease. Rob was a gem of a man and enjoyed the best days of his career at Derby. Two came on free transfers from Watford, Charlie Palmer and Eric Steele. Palmer was a quietly cheerful right-back with good pace and, after leaving Derby, had an excellent period with Notts County. Steele was an urbane goalkeeper, experienced in promotions with Peterborough, Brighton, Cardiff, on a loan spell, and Watford, where he gave way to Steve Sherwood, who could whip the ball downfield more effectively. Webb's brief span as chairman ended in August when Ian Maxwell, one of Robert's sons, took over. Webb stayed on, as managing director, while Robert Maxwell continued as Oxford's chairman, thus circumventing the League regulations about running two clubs. It was quite obvious that Maxwell senior was Derby's financial backstop, although he was always more concerned with persuading others to invest than with flinging around his own cash. For three years, the system worked brilliantly. Ian Maxwell was determined to make his own way in business but, in direct contrast to his father, had a pleasant manner, while Webb provided the knowledge about Derby and football, allowing Cox to set about building a new team. His first ace was Kevin Wilson, a striker who arrived from Banbury United in Colin Addison's time. In the relegation season, he scored only two League goals in 24 starts and eight substitute appearances but even then there was a spark to his game. He set off like a train under Cox, four goals against Hartlepool in the League Cup and a hat-trick against Bolton before a broken arm put him out. When he was fit again, Ipswich paid £150,000 for him, money that was to subsidise the purchase of Trevor Christie from Nottingham Forest and Gary Micklewhite from Queen's Park Rangers. The deal suited Ipswich too, as Wilson did well for them and they doubled their money when he moved on to Chelsea. He, too, spent time with Notts, then largely populated by former or future Rams, and, on a parental qualification, won 42 caps for Northern Ireland. Steve Cherry went to Walsall before the season began and, when Steele was injured, John Burridge joined on loan from Wolverhampton Wanderers. Cox wanted to make it permanent but Burridge preferred a move to Sheffield United and put it around that he climbed through the office window at the Raynesway training ground to escape further pressure from the Derby manager. Later in the season, Derby borrowed Steve Sutton, a former Pop-side fan who should never have been allowed to escape in the first place, from Nottingham Forest. It was possible to see a team taking shape and they finished strongly, losing only one of the last 10 League games, but the Centenary year also included the earliest FA Cup exit in Derby's history. Even the famous defeat by Boston United was in round two but in November 1984, the Rams lost 2-1 in the first round at the Victoria Ground, Hartlepool, their fifth meeting, including two-legged League Cup ties, with United in three seasons. It was not a distinguished day and former winners always attract attention when they are knocked out so early. The only further FA Cup action came in January, when Burton Albion staged their third round tie against Leicester City at the Baseball Ground. The day was soured when Burton goalkeeper Paul Evans was knocked out by a missile, probably a chunk of seating, thrown from the Osmaston End. Despite Leicester's smoothly efficient 6-1 win, featuring a hat-trick by Gary Lineker, the FA ordered the tie to be replayed behind closed doors. This took place at

Highfield Road, Coventry, and provided a weird atmosphere as Leicester won again, considerably more narrowly. Albion's manager then was Neil Warnock who, not for the last time, showed how easily he slides into contentious situations. As far as Derby were concerned, the standard of the staff was improving, with three of the first year's captures immensely important when the team took off, Hindmarch, Micklewhite and Geraint Williams. Micklewhite, playing on the right of midfield, patrolled the line with boundless energy and was one of those players, much coveted by managers, who was ready in August and did not stop running until May. He immediately set off on a sequence of 112 consecutive League games, halted only by an Achilles tendon operation, and had quality to match his consistency. Playing in an FA Cup Final, as he did for QPR, is invaluable experience to add to a developing club and he was an ideal professional. Cox was on Williams' trail for five months before Bristol Rovers parted, for £40,000, just before the 1985 deadline. Always called George at Derby, Williams added balance to midfield, not least because he could sense danger before it developed. Over the years, there were so many occasions when he appeared as the back man to impede an opposition attack. He was there to hold the departments together and, while at Derby, progressed into the Wales team. He had seven good years before joining Ipswich, where he greatly relished the Suffolk countryside and tempo of life, later becoming Colchester United's assistant-manager. All three were known quantities in that supporters, as well as management, were never let down. Even on less fruitful days, commitment could be taken as read.

Cox was aware that Derby were progressing but was keen to accelerate the process and embarked on a busy summer. The vastly experienced Mark Wallington who, in a run of seven years, chalked up 332 consecutive appearances for Leicester, was signed as the senior goalkeeper. That was an untroubled deal but the most pointed lesson of the summer was that determination was needed to talk to selling managers after the League's transfer tribunals. These were held to fix a fee when clubs were unable to agree and the selling side usually stormed out, feeling they were diddled. There were two on the same day at Villa Park and, first, Derby were told to pay £67,500 for defender Ross MacLaren when Shrewsbury wanted £125,000. While Webb called it a fair hearing, Shrewsbury manager Chic Bates said: "We have lost a good player at less than his value. They have favoured the buying side, as seems to happen in most cases." Bates was calm when set against Bolton manager Charlie Wright after a £38,000 fee was set for Jeff Chandler, well below the £100,000 they sought. Wright was apoplectic and had no intention of stopping for a reasoned comment on the decision. At Derby's third hearing of the month, they opted for a conditional tribunal over Steve McClaren's move from Hull City. That meant they could pull out if the price was over their reserve of £60,000. When the tribunal said £70,000, the deal still went through because Fred Fern, one of the directors, put his hand in his pocket. Derby spent £200,000 in the summer on four important players and released two of the higher wage earners, John Robertson, who returned to Forest, and Kenny Burns. Derby meant business and, in his cautious way, Cox said: "If every player is totally genuine with himself and with everybody else in the dressing-room and if we have a reasonable run of luck, there is no reason why we should not be involved in a strong promotion challenge. That is about as near as you will get to a forecast from me." In his final year, Taylor shot out a 'Top six by Christmas' line that was to haunt him. There was no way Cox would make that kind of rash claim, although he had a team, with Rob Hindmarch now captain, well equipped to make an impact on the Third Division. The Maxwells demanded no less.

THE BOUNCING
CZECH

NOTHING illustrated Derby County's determination to take the first step back up the League than the signing of John Gregory from Queen's Park Rangers for £100,000 in November, 1985. Arthur Cox pinned his faith on one of the new men, Steve McClaren, as the midfield creator. In early November, McClaren succumbed to a hamstring and back injury that had a worryingly long term look to it and Cox was eager to maintain the balance of a side that had recently won five League games on the trot. Gregory earned the last of his six England caps only 18 months earlier and he gave an extra edge to Derby's midfield. There was a swagger about his play, so he spread around his own confidence, and he was a mean opponent if there was anything or anybody to be sorted out. The 1985-86 season launched an exhilarating phase in the Derby County story. They were so nearly down and out in the High Court but, with Derby, there is always a chance of rehabilitation because the support is there. There will be a quorum however low the club sinks but, once convinced that good things are happening, the ranks soon swell. Cox and Roy McFarland had a side geared to promotion although, as always, nothing could be taken for granted because any division demands consistency over nine months. The points that have to be chiselled out are as important as those earned on the rare days when everything clicks. Most of the team building was done in the second half of the previous season or in summer but, in August, John Robertson returned to Nottingham Forest on a free transfer to close an episode that did not work for him or Derby. In the same month, attracting only local attention at the time, Derby signed Phil Gee from Gresley Rovers. He had been there less than a couple of months after playing for Riley Sports in his native Black Country but David Nish, then Gresley's chairman, alerted his former club. Ron Jukes, Derby's chief scout, went to have a look and returned with the message that there was a degree of urgency because others were also sniffing. Gee, slightly baffled by the speed of events, was slim, long legged and fast. He reckoned professional football was a better bet than being a painter and decorator, showing a refreshingly uncomplicated approach in his first winter with the Reserves. If there was a chance, he homed in on goal and let fly, rapidly proving that he struck the ball well while keeping it low. He scored 31 goals as the Reserves became the first Third Division club to win the Central League and it was clear that there was a natural talent.

Jeff Chandler scored twice on the opening day when Derby beat Bournemouth but blend was elusive in the early weeks as Derby won only two of their first eight League games. Hartlepool were knocked out of the League Cup after a scare at the Victoria Ground but there was more of a clue about the level they could reach when they beat Leicester City over two legs in the same competition. Some adjustments were made as Charlie Palmer replaced Floyd Streete at right-back and Geraint Williams, proving not for the last time to be a slow starter, took over from the tenacious Mickey Lewis in midfield. From that point, the Rams were more settled and a run of five consecutive League victories pushed them in the right direction. One, on a Tuesday evening at the Priestfield Stadium, Gillingham, was settled by Chandler's marvellous individual goal at the end of a great run. In 2003, I bumped into him at Deepdale before Derby subsided woefully to Preston North End and the Gillingham goal cropped up within minutes. In a way, that is unfair because Jeff scored 15 League and Cup goals that season, including the first hat-trick of his career against Telford United. He had the traditional winger's perky approach and made a significant contribution, so it was not as if that goal at Gillingham was all he achieved: but it was special. They saw plenty of Gillingham that season, a match in the Freight-Rover Trophy as well as an FA Cup tie and replay. The idea of a Cup for the lower divisions is commendable but the early exchanges were in groups of three, one home game and one away. The obvious method would have been tight regionalisation to cut the travelling but Derby were grouped with Gillingham and Brentford, which made no sense at all. They took a reserve side to Brentford, allowing Gee to make his debut, and emerged with a 0-0 draw before losing at home to Gillingham. Cox was never happy to surrender at any level but the Rams were as well out of it. They played 60 matches that season and the stress was increased by the state of the Baseball Ground pitch, which gave rise to a series of worried telephone calls whenever rain was heard on the morning of a match. After they beat Wigan Athletic on a mud-heap just before Christmas, Tony Kelly, a talented midfield player who was briefly with Derby, said: "That pitch could be the one thing to stop Derby going up." Williams did not score many goals but suddenly unleashed a rocket to salvage a point at Millmoor. Correspondents from local papers usually preserve the niceties and one who followed Rotherham United for years said at the end: "Well Derby will go up." I was about to suggest that they had not played at all well when, tight lipped, he completed the sentence – "with that kind of luck." Williams was modest about it. "They either lift out the net or finish in the street," he said, with his typical, slightly flippant, approach. Derby soon followed this with a 7-0 home win over Lincoln City and made FA Cup progress with comfortable victories over Crewe Alexandra and Telford. After winning the replay against Gillingham, they beat Sheffield United at Bramall Lane thanks to Rob Hindmarch's goal. Blades fans turned on the manager, Ian Porterfield, and there was an extraordinary sight after the game when the United chairman, Reg Brealey, stood on a low wall behind the main stand, attempting to placate very dissatisfied South Yorkshire customers. Derby held Sheffield Wednesday to a draw before going out in the fifth round replay at Hillsborough. That was on March 5 and Derby still had 19 League games to fit into the next two months.

Reading ran away with the Third Division, top from the end of August until the final table. Under Ian Branfoot, they were a direct, harrying side who made life difficult for opponents and had a trump card in Trevor Senior, responsible for 27 of their 67 goals. In the last lap, it became clear that the other two promotion places lay between Plymouth, Wigan and Derby. It was advantage Plymouth in March, when they beat the Rams 4-1 at Home Park with two goals for John Clayton, an articulate Scot who began his League career at the Baseball Ground, but that was too early to be decisive. It was, though, one of nine consecutive victories for Argyle, who finished the season with another four. That form carried them into second place on the surge after they stood eighth at the beginning of March.

Wigan and the Rams were performing more edgily. Derby depressed their fans by losing at home to Bristol Rovers in April, a game they should have won easily. The footprints on the rolled mud were significant when the teams went off at half-time, as all the action had taken place near the Rovers' penalty area. Derby hung on and, because of postponements as well as their heavy programme, had three games left when Wigan finished their season on May 3, with 83 points. Mickey Thomas, on loan from West Bromwich Albion for his experience with the likes of Manchester United, Chelsea and Wales, did not make the expected impact and Chandler was already back before the key games. Swansea City, sliding down the League as quickly as they once rose under John Toshack, were comfortably beaten 3-0 at Vetch Field to set up the home match against Rotherham United on Cup Final eve as a Baseball Ground occasion. If Derby won, they were up: anything less would leave the outcome hanging on the final game at Darlington. They did it at home, in front of 21,036, and were sparked by Gee who, as substitute for the injured Williams, repeated his Central League pattern by running at goal and smashing in a low shot. Mike Trusson equalised but what appeared a generous penalty gave Christie the chance to send Derby up. He was not the most outwardly confident of players but he mastered the tension to score convincingly. Job complete and, as the players did their lap to salute the crowd, the only sad sight was the way fans had to clamber up the cages. It was necessary to find some solution to hooliganism but fencing them in was demeaning and, as the Hillsborough FA Cup semi-final of 1989 was to show, ultimately dangerous. There were no regrets when the Baseball Ground fences disappeared soon after that awful occasion.

Promotion was hard earned and deserved. Cox spurned the word consolidation when he looked ahead to the Second Division but his signings had the stamp of players who could establish the team at a higher level. Steve Cross, an industrious midfield player, was taken from Shrewsbury Town and central defender David Linighan from Hartlepool. Linighan never appeared in Derby's first team and moved to Shrewsbury six months later. Mark Lillis was the big capture, from Manchester City with Christie going to Maine Road in part-exchange. Having faced Gillingham five times in the promotion season, so having plenty of opportunities to watch right-back Mel Sage, Derby were finally successful in signing him to be paired with Michael Forsyth, picked up from West Bromwich Albion the previous March. Forsyth, 20 when he joined Derby, was embarking on a considerable career. He had always regarded himself as a central defender but, following Steve Buckley's departure to Lincoln City, the vacancy was at left-back and, as Forsyth commented later, he picked the position up as he went along. Buckley, more of a marauder, was the one bonus to emerge from Tommy Docherty's management and, like him, Forsyth was there week after week. Buckley twice carried runs of consecutive appearances past 100 and Forsyth managed it once. Of the summer arrivals, only Sage made a lasting impact on the season and his contribution ended in February when he broke a collarbone at Roker Park, Sunderland. Lillis was an earlier casualty, suffering a knee ligaments injury in September. By the time he was fit, Bobby Davison's partnership with Gee was flourishing but the sight of Lillis on the bench remains a sharp memory of the campaign. He sat there, totally engrossed in the game but absolutely bursting to be involved: he looked as if hawsers were needed to keep him there. Inevitably, his contribution was limited but his moment came with the winner against Bradford City at the Baseball Ground in April. He rushed across to the Pop side, climbed half up the fence and demanded "How about that, then?" There are few things more deflating, after all the careful preparations, than to lose the opening game at home, as Derby did against Oldham Athletic. There were long faces after the match, supporters thinking it could be a difficult season, and the gloom deepened when, four days later, Chester City also won in the first leg of a League Cup tie. Nobody else emerged from the Baseball Ground with victory all season because Derby were about to rush straight through the Second Division. They were given extra strength in October, when Hindmarch returned after a summer cartilage operation in a 1-0 win at Shrewsbury, but even without the captain were already blending into a formidable unit. Cox was the Second Division Manager of the Month for October, an award that often blights a team's next outing. Instead, Derby celebrated by defending brilliantly at the Victoria Ground to overcome Stoke City 2-0. At times, the pressure was intense and Stoke piled into the penalty area so eagerly that several loose mauls were formed. In some ways, it typified the season because this was an honest team, happily prepared to work for each other, believing in the cause. Cox was obviously delighted with his side but worked hard to prevent it showing. He was always a man for the long view. "We don't go up in a balloon when we win and we don't jump off the bridge if we lose," he said, many times. One of his favourites was to greet victory by saying: "It's a good result only if we put another one alongside it." As soon as one game was filed away in his record books, it was time to shift the focus. Momentum developed steadily and Derby hit the front before the turn of the year. Gregory's penalty earned three points at a refurbished Valley Parade in the first game there for 19 months following the fire that swept through the main stand on their promotion day. The next day, a home win over Barnsley put Derby at the top of the table for the first time and, with no FA Cup run this time after an immediate exit at Hillsborough, they remained among the leading group from then on. It was time to emulate the days of Clough and Taylor with a significant February signing and £140,000 persuaded Watford to part with Nigel Callaghan, who emerged at Vicarage Road around the same time as John Barnes in Graham Taylor's rising side. Watford were direct and liked to put the ball in the penalty area as early as possible, with the long throw a significant weapon, but also made intelligent use of two wingers to feed the tall forwards who became a Taylor trademark. There was not much to separate Barnes and Callaghan in the early days, both good on the ball, able to hit accurate centres and score goals, but Barnes was the one who reached the top. The Jamaican had a harder kernel of ambition, while half of Callaghan wanted to be a disc jockey. Derby had used Graham Harbey on the left and, although he did a good job, his inclinations tended towards his defensive duties. Callaghan added flair and imagination, soon proving his worth with the only goal of the game to beat Millwall at the Den. He also scored in a 2-0 victory at Ipswich, a game notable for Mark Wallington's courage. The goalkeeper, steadiness itself since the start of the season, had a hand broken in the first half as he took the ball off the former Derby player, Kevin Wilson. He was in considerable pain but Cox did not summon the doctor during the interval in case Ipswich were alerted. Wallington managed to disguise the severity of the injury and complete the game with the goalkeepers' cherished clean sheet. Cox ran on at the end to show his appreciation but it was Wallington's last senior game for the Rams. In the short term, they had Eric Steele as experienced cover and before their return to the First Division, they signed Peter Shilton. There was soon a Cox salute for Steele after an inspired display against Huddersfield at the Baseball Ground and the Rams were able to clinch promotion at home with two games to spare when they beat Leeds United. It was a long way from the fearsome Leeds teams produced by Don Revie but that failed to dilute supporters' pleasure. After defeat by Reading at Elm Park, where they never made an impression, Derby took the title with a grandstand finish, three goals in the last 10 minutes to beat Plymouth 4-2. As it happened, they did not need the points because Portsmouth, the only other team with a chance, lost to Sheffield United but it was a great way to go out. Dave Smith, the Plymouth manager, stood in the tunnel afterward, watching and savouring what he knew to be a great occasion in a football town.

Derby were worth watching throughout the season because they had the blend right, good players who were prepared to work as a team. There was always experience in goal and, once Rob Hindmarch returned in place of the admirable Dick Pratley, a natural leader in defence. Hindmarch's first instinct was to attack the ball while Ross MacLaren cruised around to pick up the pieces. The full-backs, Mel Sage until he was injured, Paul

Blades and Michael Forsyth did their jobs in differing styles and there was an equally effective unit in midfield. Geraint Williams was at the hub of it, doing the simple things or, as Ron Atkinson frequently says, the ugly things, by making sure opponents did not have a clear run while John Gregory looked after the creative side, while leaving a foot in occasionally. "John improved our passing," said Cox, who then added some flair by signing Nigel Callaghan. Gary Micklewhite, who did not miss a match in the successive promotions, was one of the heroes. Not long after he joined Derby, I had to show Micklewhite a book in which Alan Mullery, once his manager with Queen's Park Rangers, accused him of being a bad professional. It was probably libellous but, having looked at the offending passage, Micklewhite said: "I would be more upset if it came from somebody other than Mullery." He did not ask to borrow the book and it was a startling allegation because, for eight years and 288 games at Derby, Micklewhite was an absolute diamond, always where his manager needed him to be even if Cox allowed himself the occasional grumble about a shortage of goals. Mark Lillis, like Trevor Christie in the Third Division, was essentially a target-man but injury to Lillis forced a rethink. Bobby Davison and Phil Gee were alert strikers with pace, both wanting to run on to passes. Davison was good at popping up in penalty areas, while the characteristic Gee goal came from a low shot following a strong run. They worried defenders and were responsible for 34 goals between them as Derby played to them perfectly, with Gregory adding a dozen. It was a team in which nobody hid or shirked responsibility and was impeccably managed by Arthur Cox, with Roy McFarland and Gordon Guthrie at his side. They did not need all the supernumeraries who, in recent years, have made benches such crowded areas, not only at Derby. With First Division football assured just over three years after the High Court appearances, an expected announcement was made at the end of May. Robert Maxwell resigned as Oxford United's chairman to take over from his son Ian at Derby. Another son, Kevin, stepped up at the Manor Ground and, although the regulations were observed, it was obvious that father controlled two clubs, as he already had done for three years. Having said that, Ian was justly popular at Derby and, as was discovered before too

Champions again. Derby County with the Football League Championship trophy they won in 1974-75 under Dave Mackay (pictured second from the left of the back row). Third from the right of the back row is Peter Daniel, who for most of the season stood in magnificently for the injured Roy McFarland.

In 1977, Derby County asked Brian Clough to leave Nottingham Forest and return to the Baseball Ground as manager once more. Clough came back, followed by a trail of hopeful supporters, but, alas, only to deliver in person his reasons for staying at the City Ground.

Tommy Docherty took over from Colin Murphy, who lost his job in the most shameful of circumstances. Docherty was soon busy in the transfer market with players coming and going with alarming regularity.

New Rams chairman Mike Watterson, who had made his money through the development of snooker, greets Archie Gemmill, star of two Derby County title-winning teams, now re-signed for the Rams by Peter Taylor.

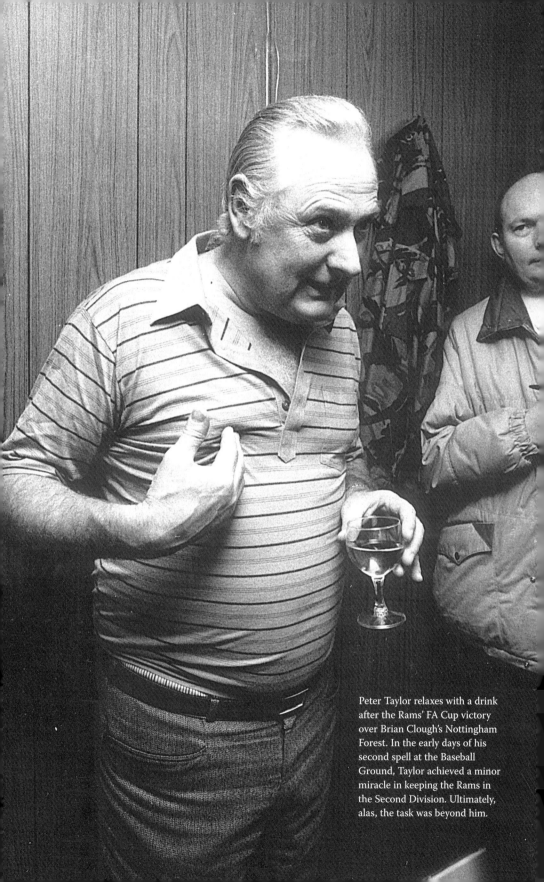

Peter Taylor relaxes with a drink after the Rams' FA Cup victory over Brian Clough's Nottingham Forest. In the early days of his second spell at the Baseball Ground, Taylor achieved a minor miracle in keeping the Rams in the Second Division. Ultimately, alas, the task was beyond him.

The Rams' centenary year of 1984 could hardly have been worse, relegated to the Third Division and on the brink of bankruptcy. Stuart Webb worked tirelessly to avert disaster and eventually persuaded Robert Maxwell, seen here with Webb and Maxwell' son Ian, to save the club. Little did we know that Maxwell himself would eventually face huge financial problems.

It was quite a coup for relegated Derby County to bring in the former Newcastle manager Arthur Cox. The new man responded by taking the Rams from the Third Division to the First in successive seasons. Cox eventually succumbed to a back problem which prevented him from working, but not before he had become Derby's longest-serving manager since George Jobey.

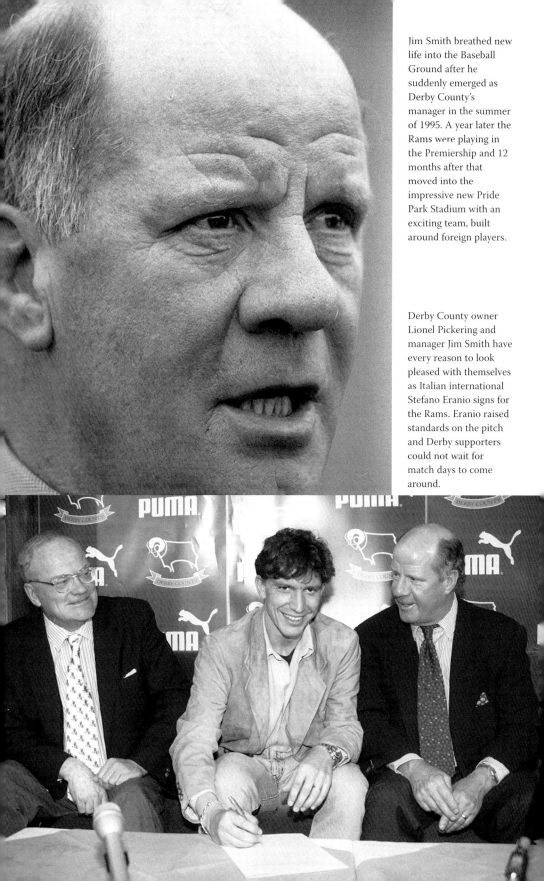

Jim Smith breathed new life into the Baseball Ground after he suddenly emerged as Derby County's manager in the summer of 1995. A year later the Rams were playing in the Premiership and 12 months after that moved into the impressive new Pride Park Stadium with an exciting team, built around foreign players.

Derby County owner Lionel Pickering and manager Jim Smith have every reason to look pleased with themselves as Italian international Stefano Eranio signs for the Rams. Eranio raised standards on the pitch and Derby supporters could not wait for match days to come around.

After Smith had been sacked and Derby had dallied with Colin Todd, John Gregory, a former Rams player, took over. At first it seemed as though he might rescue the club from relegation from the Premiership but the damage had already been done. As a miserable season in the First Division drew to a close, Gregory himself was dismissed in the most controversial of circumstances. Derby fans were suffering again and, of course, by now, I was 'just a supporter' once more.

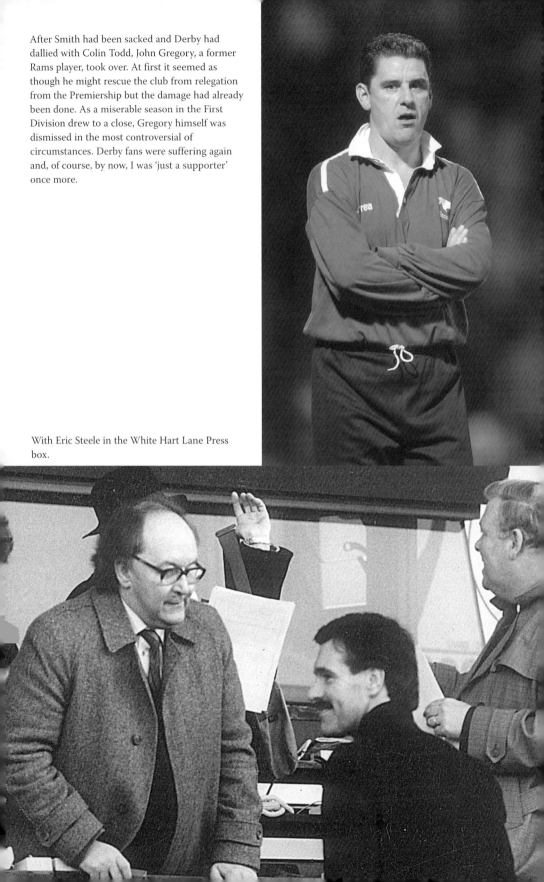

With Eric Steele in the White Hart Lane Press box.

With David Nish and Linda McFarland at a Former Players dinner.

Frank Upton introduced me to George Darwin (right) one of my favourite players.

Mike Lowe, then editor of the *Derby Evening Telegraph*, presents a tankard to mark 25 years at the paper. I am asking him about the absence of an apostrophe.

My farewell party at Pride Park: from left – John Morris, Roy McFarland, Dave Mackay, the author, Gordon Guthrie, Colin Boulton, Steve Powell, and John O'Hare.

long, acted as an essential buffer zone. Stuart Webb, who tailed Maxwell so assiduously in 1984, was delighted. "In football terms, it is akin to signing Diego Maradona," he said. At the time, the comparison may not have been too far fetched because Maxwell was ambitious and craved publicity, especially through the columns of the *Daily Mirror*, which he then owned. He was also, again at the time, extremely wealthy and Webb envisaged the kind of dictatorship practised in Italy by Agnelli or Berlusconi. Maxwell's domineering personality meant there would always be difficulties: Webb hoped they would be worth it but discovered he had to control a bull elephant. Ultimately, it was impossible and Derby supporters came to detest Maxwell.

The *Derby Telegraph* had run a series of player profiles, spread across two pages, to reflect interest in the club and it was felt similar treatment of Maxwell was in order. The arrangements were made so the photographer, Mike Inman, and I set off for Headington Hill Hall, close to Oxford United's ground. That meant time for a gentle lunch in Woodstock but the first snag arose when we reported to the gatehouse outside Maxwell's council-owned estate, which he occupied at a peppercorn rent. The great man was not there and, indeed, had not been seen all weekend but they were kind enough to establish that he was at the *Mirror* headquarters in Holborn. The fact that I was booked in to see Maxwell earned a spot in the underground car park, a huge advantage in central London, and a ride in the only lift that stopped at his floor. There were plenty waiting on leather settees for audience, many with faces vaguely remembered from television news bulletins, union leaders and the like. Eventually, most of them were hustled off and told to make new appointments because, Maxwell boomed, "I have to see my friends from Derby." As soon as we were in the presence, Maxwell turned on the television news at a sufficiently high volume as to make conversation impossible. Once satisfied, he settled with us and his attendant Press Officer, there to make sure his master was not misquoted. Maxwell was imposing, the kind of man who filled a room through personality as well as bulk, and at the beginning of his relationship with Derby, I was unlikely to lob in any hand grenades. There was promise for the club because his first action was to sign Peter

Shilton from Southampton. The cost of the deal was grossly exaggerated in the *Mirror* but that worried few because, at the age of 37, Shilton was demonstrably the best goalkeeper in the country, if not the world, and his achievements with Nottingham Forest were still fresh in the mind. Mark Wright, also from Southampton, followed in August, after the season started, but it was a more complicated deal because Maxwell was on his yacht and quibbling about the fee. The secretary, Michael Dunford, tried to fill the time by showing Wright houses in the area but was near the end of his repertoire and heading into the Peak District by the time Maxwell agreed that the deal should proceed. Wright was like a thoroughbred horse, a great mover around the centre of defence but always restless and highly-strung. Both the new men captained England as Derby players, something that had not happened since Tommy Cooper and Jack Barker in the 1930s, and their arrival was essential in Derby's survival in 1987-88. Then, as now, the first season is the most difficult and the lesson for a team battling to survive is to bring in good defenders. That principle served Jim Smith well when, on a shorter term basis, he signed first Paul McGrath, then Taribo West. And, of course, Brian Clough and Peter Taylor made good defenders the prerequisite for clubs seeking success.

So far, Maxwell was in credit but two particular episodes in 1987-88 revealed how difficult it would be to control his erratic nature. In November, he wanted to buy Watford from Elton John, who was keen to be free of his obligations. Maxwell tried to justify something that obviously flew in the face of League regulations by pointing out that BPCC, his major printing company, was a leading employer in Watford but that reasoning failed to carry conviction. While the League had been prepared to accept the obvious link between Derby and Oxford United, this was a step too far, so they objected. As a result, Maxwell threatened to walk away from football, a prospect that greatly worried other members of the Derby board as they would be presented with a considerable financial liability. It was also unfortunate timing for Cox, who had just sold Bobby Davison to Leeds United for £350,000. Reservations about Davison arose following a knee ligaments operation and the clear intention at the time was to put the fee towards a replacement. Instead, while Maxwell had a froth about the

League's Mismanagement Committee, a term he was rather pleased to have coined, Derby were not in the market. Once this was out of the way, Cox agreed a £400,000 fee with Liverpool for Paul Walsh, a lively and tenacious striker who would have suited them admirably. The deal then depended on Maxwell making contact with Liverpool chairman Sir John Smith but, because he was so dilatory, Tottenham Hotspur nipped in to take Walsh. Retrospective suspicion about that arose 18 months later when Maxwell, by then clearly tired of Derby, helped to fund Tottenham's purchase of Gary Lineker. The worst episode occurred in April, 1988, when, through the *Daily Mirror*, Maxwell revealed that he had invited Johan Cruyff to become Derby's Director of Football. It was shameful as neither Cox nor Stuart Webb, the managing director, knew anything about it until the story appeared. Cox was both livid and deeply offended at a time when Derby had it all on to survive in Division One. He felt he was being undervalued and issued a statement, telling Maxwell to behave himself, but a kernel of suspicion entered the relationship. And, of course, like so many 'exclusives' the story simply withered and died. It was a hard slog in 1987-88, although Derby were off on the right foot with an opening day victory over Luton Town. Also off that day, within five minutes of the first whistle, was Luton's intimidating centre-forward Mick Harford. Eric Steele moved to Southend United in the summer and was cordially welcomed when he returned to the Baseball Ground for a League Cup tie, in which he kept a clean sheet to eliminate the Rams over two legs. FA Cup interest was equally brief, a third round exit at home to Chelsea, but the League season began reasonably well, with Derby in the top half by the end of November. The most memorable day was at Newcastle in November, Cox's first return since he steered United to promotion. Because St James' Park was being developed, changing facilities were temporarily housed in a corner of the Leazes End so, instead of being able to slip up the tunnel into the dug-out, Cox had to go right along one goal-line and half-way up the touchline in front of the vacant main stand. He was cheered and applauded all the way in one of the most emotional welcomes I have ever heard as the Geordies acknowledged he gave them a square deal as well as good players. He was expecting a good reception but was deeply touched by the fervour of it. After that, Peter Shilton gave a stupendous exhibition of goalkeeping and one Newcastle fan observed to the Press box, also in temporary accommodation, that if the goalie was not marked 10 out of 10, none of us knew what had happened on the field. Without Shilton, Derby would have been beaten out of sight and it looked as if his brilliance might be in vain when Paul Goddard, in space, met a centre with his head. He did everything right, a good contact to send the ball towards the bottom corner, and still Shilton saved. At that moment, Newcastle seemed to realise they were never going to beat a great 'keeper at the peak of his powers. Every early point was vital because, while the Watford affair rumbled, Derby hit the skids with eight consecutive League defeats that took them down to 18th. It was a dangerous position as, with a First Division of 21 clubs in phase one of a reduction, three were relegated and fourth from the bottom, which turned out to be Chelsea, had to take part in the Play-offs. Ted McMinn, signed from Seville at the end of January, was limited by injury to seven matches but, even when out of action, was good for morale. The winger, who arrived from Spain with a savage cut across one knee, had his eccentricities and, in his home debut against Manchester United, pushed the ball past the full-back and ran outside the linesman before collecting it. In that brief spell, he promised entertaining skill and even more important at the time was the return of Rob Hindmarch, omitted since August. Wright welcomed his new partner who would, he knew, go to the ball as soon as it came into dangerous areas: the defence was suddenly more reliable and, on reflection, Hindmarch should have been in sooner. The run of defeats ended at Oxford with a fraught 0-0 and, from then on, Derby put together enough points to stay clear of trouble, helped by the arrival of Frank Stapleton on a short contract from Ajax Amsterdam. The former Arsenal and Manchester United striker underwent back surgery while in Holland and needed games to be ready for the Republic of Ireland's appearance in the European Championship finals. It suited all parties because Stapleton, although short of full match fitness, knew where to stand and what to do, apart from being the most quotable of stars. He was a focal point, enabling Gregory to drop back into midfield.

Cox's confrontation with Maxwell paid dividends in the summer of 1988, when significant money was available, but the manager was disappointed by Gregory's decision to join Portsmouth as coach. Cox believed the midfield player had another year or two of football in him. "John found 1987-88 tiring," said Cox, "but we all did. We had to go flat out in every game." Ross MacLaren was also on the way out and Swindon Town appeared to have a bargain at £150,000. Too much of a bargain, as it turned out, because Swindon failed to reveal the full details of his contract to a tribunal and Derby later received a further £25,000. Swindon, found guilty of making unauthorised payments, were deprived of the First Division place they had earned through the 1989-90 Play-offs. John Chiedozie joined Derby on a free transfer from Tottenham and, although a speedy winger at his best, soon succumbed to further injuries. Paul Goddard, from Newcastle United for £425,000 was a more exciting capture, a centre-forward able to hold the ball and score his share of goals. Cox, conscious of Derby's recent past, called him his John O'Hare: his Kevin Hector was to arrive in October. Nick Pickering, a versatile left-sided player from Coventry City with an England cap and an FA Cup winners' medal, cost £250,000 but, like so many of Derby's signings from Highfield Road, it did not work out. Maxwell was also looking abroad, towards Czechoslovakian internationals Ivo Knoflicek and Lubos Kubik, who walked out of a Slavia Prague tour in West Germany and sought asylum. It was a *Daily Mirror* exclusive as the players were taken to a safe house in Spain but any transfer was sure to be difficult. As with all players from behind the Iron Curtain, they were technically amateurs but FIFA and UEFA saw chaos ahead if the pair were allowed to pick up their careers in another country after walking away from Slavia. It was long before the influx of foreign players into England but Derby could probably have signed them had they been prepared to pay fees. Knoflicek and Kubik were introduced at a Press conference, held in London the following January, and taken on the Baseball Ground pitch to wave to supporters. Kubik, especially, could have been a major asset in midfield, strong and elegant as he was to show in Italy with Fiorentina. That move came about after FIFA's decision in April, 1989, that Knoflicek and Kubik were professionals, so had to return to their club until a regulation transfer agreement was concluded. Indirectly, the episode clarified the status of footballers behind the Iron Curtain and Kubik was still in the Czech Republic squad for the European Championships in England in 1996. It was far more straightforward to sign Trevor Hebberd from Oxford, with Mickey Lewis going in part-exchange. Hebberd, outstanding when Oxford beat Queen's Park Rangers in the Milk Cup Final, was a stylish midfield player, lean and upright. He could add a few goals, as he soon demonstrated with stunning effect against Newcastle.

Mark Wallington's departure to Lincoln City and the sale of Andy Garner to Blackpool hardly balanced the books but they left with thanks for their contribution while the turnover of the squad was maintained. Talks to bring in striker Lee Chapman from French club Niort came to nothing and, as he later revealed in an autobiography, he was not convinced about the sincerity of Derby's offer. Cox was also in demand as Leeds and Newcastle sought new managers but decided to stay at Derby, as he had when Aston Villa came calling. Apart from any contractual considerations, he had a good thing going at the Baseball Ground and it looked a whole lot better in October, 1988, when Dean Saunders became Derby's first £1m capture. The football world wondered about the deal with Oxford because, in effect, it was as if Maxwell transferred a considerable cheque from one capacious trouser pocket to the other. No complaint was made, except by Oxford manager Mark Lawrenson, who was not involved in the discussions. Within days, he was sacked by Kevin Maxwell and Saunders scored twice in a thrilling debut against Wimbledon. Cox had his Hector and Saunders, a Welsh international once given a free transfer from Swansea by John Bond, was a natural hero at the Baseball Ground. He scored goals, was full of life around the club and clearly enjoyed playing. A smile was never far away at Derby but when he moved to Liverpool, it was a different Dean. He looked uncomfortable and returned to his previous manager for advice because he never felt others at Anfield accepted him. There were more big transfers, along with 75 Welsh caps, for him, to Aston Villa, Galatasaray, Nottingham Forest, Sheffield United and Benfica before he wound down with Bradford City.

He was leading scorer in each of his three seasons with Derby and seldom missed a game.

Derby won eight away games in 1988-89 and conceded only 38 goals as they finished fifth, comfortably their best since Dave Mackay's last full season as manager 13 years earlier. They had a spine built around Shilton, Wright, the supporters' Player of the Year, and Saunders. With them, Cox had good players who were willing workers and it was a considerable feat of management for him and Roy McFarland. In the space of three years, they went from the Third Division to European qualification: the only snag was that there was no Europe for English clubs, in exile as a result of the Heysel disaster in which lives were lost before the European Cup Final between Liverpool and Juventus. Derby were never going to win the title but they were competitive throughout the season. There were victories to savour, 3-1 over Spurs at White Hart Lane when the flying McMinn scored twice, 2-0 at Old Trafford and best of all, considering the state of the Championship race, 2-1 over Arsenal at Highbury in May, illuminated by a glorious goal when Saunders swept in Williams' angled pass. That kept the pressure on Arsenal, who took the title by the narrowest of margins by winning their final game at Liverpool. Strangely, a defeat sticks in the memory. Before they went to Plough Lane, with its abysmal facilities and aggressive stewards, Derby had conceded only six goals in 10 away games but Wimbledon startled them by winning 4-0. Nor did it stem from traditional Wimbledon methods, bang the ball in the box and fight for it, but came through excellent football played at high pace. Paul Miller hit three but Terry Phelan, up and down the left like a jack rabbit, stood out. Lawrie Sanchez never missed a chance to sneer at those who did not love Wimbledon and was, therefore, seldom silent but they were absolutely brilliant that night. Peter Shilton summed up the season most aptly when he said it was a battling fifth. Having won the title with Forest, Shilton knew that Derby had to be strengthened if they were to take the next step. So did Cox, who said the Rams were at a crossroads, a comment indicating he had a fair idea which direction they would take.

Robert Maxwell missed the next annual meeting because he was in New York. He, too, was at a crossroads and about to overstretch himself financially by moving into the American publishing market. He was on the way to ruin and, during the journey, burgled the pension funds he was supposed to administer. By the time he slipped, or was pushed, off his yacht in the Atlantic, Maxwell was close to being exposed as a major fraudster. The one mercy is that he had left Derby by then. Ian Maxwell conveyed an unwelcome message to the 1989 annual meeting, that it may be necessary to sell players to balance the books. The family had, he said, kept Derby County going for five years: "Without us, you're dead." It was overwhelming arrogance but the threat gained substance when, at the end of December, 1989, Paul Goddard was sold to Millwall for £800,000. Goddard hated life at the Den – "the absolute pits," he called it later – and was relieved to be able to escape to Ipswich Town before too long. Cox was able to replace him with Mick Harford, from Luton Town for £500,000, but it was his only signing in two years. Harford was one of the toughest of centre-forwards and, although gently spoken off the field, had eyes that could look right through people. He was good company but, emphatically, not a man to cross. The team was developing holes, hastened by knee ligament injuries to Ted McMinn, at White Hart Lane when he fell awkwardly on the slight slope just outside the touchline, Gary Micklewhite and Steve Cross. Maxwell paid his first 1989-90 visit to the Baseball Ground on March 26, entering 10 minutes late after his helicopter trip and leaving with the best part of half-an-hour to go. It was close to a calculated insult but supporters did not waste the available 53 minutes, giving him frightful stick. Against all the evidence, Maxwell appeared surprised that the people of Derby did not love him and it was the beginning of the end. In summer, Rob Hindmarch went to Wolverhampton and Paul Blades to Norwich, leaving an immediate defensive hole as neither was replaced. A week into the season, Maxwell announced, at a Press conference about *The European* newspaper, that he was selling his football interests, control of Derby and Oxford plus shares in Reading dating from the Thames Valley Royals fiasco. When asked why this announcement was not made months earlier, to allow clubs time, one of his Press officers said there would have been no point in the summer because everybody was thinking about cricket. 'Stuff you' fingers were being waved from the Maxwell camp and, as he wanted £8m for Derby, there was no rush of prospective buyers. After Derby were destroyed by Paul Gascoigne's brilliant hat-trick for Spurs, a further barb was hurled towards the Baseball Ground. Through one of his companies and by way of the Spurs football chairman Irving Scholar, Maxwell advanced £1.1m to them, very useful when there was a payment due on Gary Lineker's transfer from Barcelona. Derby were in limbo and the playing season went from bad to worse. Shilton and Wright, stars of England's progress to the semi-finals in the 1990 World Cup in Italy, were still there, as was Saunders, but it was an increasing struggle to raise a team around them and the atmosphere in the club was awful, hard though management and players tried to maintain morale. A 7-1 home defeat by Liverpool confirmed what we knew already, that First Division days were fading fast, and before the game that would clinch relegation, against Manchester City at Maine Road, Maxwell, from New York, announced that Wright and Saunders were for sale. Once more, the announcement was not made through the club and when Alex Ferguson was informed of it, he remarked: "I wonder if he's told his manager." People in football knew the score and, for the way he treated the club, Maxwell was held in total contempt around Derby.

Lionel Pickering expressed an interest in taking over the club for £3m but his offer was ignored and he was even banned from the Baseball Ground. Maxwell could not be bothered to examine the bid with any care and that was typical of his high-handed attitude. Peter Gadsby, one of the bidders, was persuaded to join with the board consortium led by Brian Fearn and, in July, Maxwell finally left. So, by then, had Wright (£2.2m) and Saunders (£2.9m), both signed by Liverpool. They spoke with feeling of the good days at Derby, their relationship with Cox and their gratitude to the fans. Nobody then turned down Liverpool but, in separate interviews, they made it clear they would have been happier had the Rams continued to develop. Maxwell was unable to attend the final Press conference, where it was announced, to scornful laughter, that his helicopter had developed a fault and no replacement was available. Taking over his shares cost the new board £3,222,238.60 – with a general assumption that he would not allow the odd 60p to be forgotten – so there was little of the transfer money to play with and Cox, having been so close to the summit of the English game, had to start again. People like Maxwell have their attractions because, at the start of his involvement, he had massive financial clout, but it is always hard to persuade supporters that self-interest is not the governing motive. Derby had some good things out of Maxwell but, in the end, were left trying to pick up the pieces yet again. Maxwell did not have long to live and, in November, was found drowned near Tenerife after disappearing from his yacht. The circumstances have never been explained satisfactorily, although his financial plight soon became clear, but Derby people, despite having seen little of Robert Maxwell, felt they were close to an international news story.

BARNETT YEARS

WHEN Arthur Cox reached his peak at the Baseball Ground in 1989, Kim Barnett's heights with Derbyshire were coming close. Trophies are rare visitors to the County Ground but Derbyshire won the Sunday League in 1990, then the Benson and Hedges Cup in 1993. The first came from a sustained effort over a season but the Bensons was more startling because it was achieved without an overseas player. Ian Bishop who, but for injuries, might have become one of the greatest of all West Indian fast bowlers was ruled out early in the season. Because he played once before pulling up, that was that for Derbyshire: there were none of the temporary replacements who now slip in and out of the county game. So a long period of patient team building culminated in one of the finest Derbyshire teams but, being Derbyshire, it then began to break up and the number of players who opted to continue their careers elsewhere was a considerable irritation to supporters. The bold decision to appoint Barnett, at the age of 22, to succeed Barry Wood as captain paid off handsomely and if he was the visible leader on the field, the structure off the field was, until near the end of his reign, excellent. For a start, Philip Russell as coach had an invaluable knack of being able to identify potential in often unlikely places. There were two supportive cricket chairmen, first Charlie Elliott, then Guy Willatt. Elliott played for Derbyshire from 1932 to 1953 before becoming one of the best umpires. He stood in 42 Tests and his knowledge was as great as his status in the game. Willatt, Derbyshire's captain from 1951 to 1954, spent 25 years as a headmaster before retiring to live near Repton and his love of cricket was as vital as his ability to handle people. Barnett was both backed and respected in what became a golden era for the county. He listened to the people around him and developed into an outstanding player while annexing Denis Smith's county batting records. Barnett arrived as a middle order batsman whose leg spin was thought to be his greatest strength. From there, he became an England opener and although a highly individual technique made some critics suspicious, he was worth many more than his four Tests. Wood's abrupt departure in 1983 left Derbyshire in disarray and they were totally outplayed in three successive Championship games. In the second of them, Roger Finney's 71 did much to improve morale because, although it did not avert an innings defeat by Essex, Finney's batting showed what could be achieved by application. In the end, as experienced players and learners worked together, Derbyshire won seven Championship games, a total bettered only once, under Derek Morgan in 1966, in 20 seasons. Barnett's decision, at the end of July, to open with Iain Anderson, was a key element, as was the impact made by Ole Mortensen, the first Dane to play county cricket.

Mortensen was recommended by Ian Buxton, a former captain who had a regular coaching engagement in Denmark. When Mortensen arrived at the start of the season, Wood was asked for an immediate impression and said: "He's not as fast as I'd been led to believe." It was an extraordinary reply, suggesting Wood felt every development was part of a widespread conspiracy against him. Buxton never promised blistering pace but he had seen a bowler with a big heart, a command of line and length and an ability to move the ball away from the right hander. Mortensen, capped in 1986, spent 12 seasons in England and was often the most traditional Derbyshire bowler on view, quick enough to be awkward, persistent and seldom wasting his energy on bouncers. He took 434 wickets at the very respectable average of 23.88, was mean in one-day cricket and a character who engaged readily with supporters. He carried on a running dialogue with umpires, who never took offence at gestures to see if they were awake after turning down an lbw appeal because there was no harm meant. As he fielded on the boundary, out of the way if possible,

Mortensen chatted happily to spectators as he towelled himself during a bowling spell and kept the 12th man alert in ferrying drinks. When he had a benefit, he sheepishly dressed as a Viking during his collections and was liable to send his helpers for another circuit if there was not enough money in the buckets. One of his best games was at Abbeydale Park in his first season when, on a sub-standard pitch, he took 11 wickets in Derbyshire's first victory over Yorkshire since 1957. Bob Taylor had waited throughout his career for this moment and produced the champagne he always put in the back of his car to be ready for this occasion. It could be that the same bottles had made many fruitless trips. Michael Holding, due to join Derbyshire after the World Cup, was limited by an injury sustained in a crowd invasion at Lord's and was not properly fit until mid-August. Then one of the greatest fast bowlers the world has ever seen treated Derbyshire to his hypnotically fluent approach to the crease, so quiet that one non-striking opener did not realise the match had started until the ball was on its way. He was a joy to watch and to know. Holding is a man without affectation, fitting easily into any dressing-room as his record and personality commanded respect. Television subsequently realised the value of his deep voice with the captivating Jamaican accent although, when he encountered fellow West Indians after a day's play, the conversation became impossible to follow for anybody without the patois. He later produced an autobiography and, at the launch in London, I asked him to sign my copy. He did so willingly, including 'Thanks for your support'. That was touching, as he was already at the summit before joining Derbyshire, but typical of his kindness.

At the end of July, 1984, the incomparable Bob Taylor announced, while Derbyshire were playing in Swansea, that he would retire at the end of the season. Away games after that were emotional for the wicketkeeper as cricket followers around the country took their opportunities to say farewell to a man who always graced the game. There was especially warm applause at Taunton but the affection for Taylor ran round the country, a recognition of high skill mixed with modesty, dignity and his approach to cricket. John Hampshire retired at the same time, ending three years with Derbyshire after the bulk of his career was spent with Yorkshire, where the fuss and controversy surrounding Geoffrey Boycott pained him greatly. Like Taylor, Hampshire had firm principles on how cricket should be conducted and became one of the most reliable umpires, always ready for a chat after play.

Derbyshire were short of bowlers in 1984, when Holding was with the West Indians, Mortensen was injured and Leslaine Lambert, engaged from Guyana, never took up his contract because of knee surgery. In some matches, the overseas slot was occupied by Devon Malcolm, a 21-year-old fast bowler who was born in Jamaica but had already spent much of his life in Sheffield and gained fame by uprooting Boycott's stumps in a pre-season match. Derbyshire were already taking steps to establish a residential qualification and, after a few games, directed him towards an optician when Russell decided that a long, weaving approach to the stumps looked out of control because of an inability to see the far end clearly. He needed a new prescription for his spectacles and from that beginning emerged one of the most widely recognised sportsmen in England. He could bowl very fast and, when Holding was back with the county, was encouraged to concentrate on that aspect: control would come later. Malcolm played in 40 Tests and hit his peak in 1994 with nine for 57 in South Africa's second innings at the Oval. When he rang home that evening, his wife Jenny produced one of the great put-downs by talking about the children and shopping before asking: "What sort of a day did you have?" She knew perfectly well, of course, and, in a close family, was immensely proud. When England went to South Africa in 1995-96, Nelson Mandela greeted him as 'The Destroyer' but that was to remain the highlight of his tour. Attempts to change his bowling style at such an advanced stage of his career were doomed to failure, causing Malcolm only distress and uncertainty. Something similar happened to Andrew Harris on an England A tour and he struggled throughout the following summer. Although the most serene of individuals, Malcolm returned from that trip bitterly disillusioned. I thought he would fade quickly when he passed 30 but he was still bowling fast for Leicestershire at 40, having left Derbyshire in 1997 for a spell with Northamptonshire. His fitness, love of the game and, perhaps most important of all, pride in his performances, kept him going but, as the century came to an end, far too many gifted players were leaving Derbyshire.

In the 1980s, they were more concerned with creating a team and some later to make significant contributions entered quietly. One such was Allan Warner, a fast-medium bowler engaged from Worcestershire for 1985. He did not perform especially well for a few seasons and, indeed, offered to tear up his contract after heavy punishment in the closing overs of a 1986 Benson and Hedges quarter-final against Kent. Wisely, Derbyshire maintained their faith and, just by plenty of work in the middle, Warner became an integral part of the attack, especially at the death in limited-overs cricket. Before he left in 1996, Barnett used to refer to him respectfully as a tradesman and if his bowling was increasingly steady, his batting was occasionally explosive. For such a slight man, Warner hit the ball prodigious distances, if not always in the direction anticipated by fielders. He appeared to have a circular bat and the billowing, top-edged hook that sailed wide of third man became almost a trademark shot. He turned a few one-day games and, in 1986, was close to a Championship century against Leicestershire at Queen's Park. He flailed away happily, five sixes and nine fours, but as he neared the 90s, seemed to notice the scoreboard for the first time and tried to make sure. Inevitably, he tied up and we had to be content with a bar-emptying 91 from 90 balls. John Morris, who made his debut as a teenager in 1982, could not do much quietly, even if he tried, but needed time to turn glimpses of promise into a more substantial contribution. It was always likely to happen because, of all the English-born batsmen to play for Derbyshire, he was the most naturally gifted, even if Barnett became the most formidable. From his early days, Morris went to the crease with a strut, as if indicating to the crowd that they had better pay attention because something worth watching was on the way. Very often it was but the danger came when Morris was on top and minor lapses led to an unnecessary dismissal. He often left us wanting more but it was sad when he left for Durham after the 1993 season. He ended a fine career with Nottinghamshire, announcing his retirement before scoring two centuries in a run-filled game at Derby. The most startling entry into county cricket was by Martin Jean-Jacques, an electrician who played club cricket for Shepherd's Bush and represented Buckinghamshire in the Minor Counties competition. On his debut at Abbeydale, he batted at number 11 and scored 73 in a county record last-wicket partnership of 132 with Alan Hill. In his fourth game, he took eight for 77 in Kent's first innings at Derby and while unlikely to maintain that level, had soon disposed of the rounds at the bar which traditionally mark career-best performances. When Warner was similarly caught, colleagues aware that he had no reputation as a free spender ensured there were plenty of glasses to be filled. Warner moaned about the cost, which he quoted to the last penny, for several seasons. The most unlikely record of 1986 was set against Cornwall in the NatWest Trophy when Hill and Anderson put on 286 for the second wicket. It is fair to say that neither was a natural dasher but the Cornish bowling asked few questions, even when they overcame 30 conceded in wides. Arthur Jepson, then retired as a full-time umpire but still good for a lugubrious aside, began the day with a flurry of signals which gently died away. When asked if the bowlers had found a line, Jepson replied: "No. I packed up widing them or we'd have been here all bloody night." Hill retired at the end of 1986, to concentrate on coaching, when he probably had another year or two in him. He was the most determined of batsmen, even if his stance evolved in strange ways, and earned great respect among County players. The great West Indian fast bowler Malcolm Marshall always remembered Hill's century with a cracked kneecap and, before meetings with Hampshire, inevitably asked 'Where's Bud?' Hill was a successful Second team coach, rather less comfortable when he stepped up, and also acted as temporary secretary before Derbyshire dismissed him. He deserved better treatment but the club was in considerable disarray at the time. Geoff Miller joined Essex after the 1986 season and, despite his 34 Tests, left a feeling that he had not fully realised his potential. He returned for a second spell and developed a successful career as an after-dinner speaker before he was appointed an England selector.

When a season opens in glorious weather, it is often a false promise, as the wet summer of 1987 confirmed. For three days in April, Queen's Park, Chesterfield, was perfect, not least because Derbyshire beat Sussex by nine wickets after Bruce Roberts hit 184 from 188 balls. Roberts, a shy and reserved Northern Rhodesian who drove with immense power, went on to have a good enough summer to suggest a prosperous future. He had eight seasons with Derbyshire, averaging over 30, but did not advance as far as was hoped, in part because there was a tendency round the club to highlight weaknesses rather than concentrate on his strengths. More than many, he needed reassurance. Bernie Maher, who appeared the obvious successor to Bob Taylor, had to overcome a challenge from Chris Marples before establishing himself but, in 1987, was top of the national list with 76 dismissals. As Derbyshire finished sixth in the Championship and were in Sunday contention until the last round of matches, the team was improving markedly, while the Second XI, under Alan Hill, won the Bain Dawes Trophy. Being Derbyshire, however, there was an undercurrent and, in April, Roger Pearman left after five-and-a-half years as chief executive. It was said to be by mutual consent but few ever take that term at face value and Pearman also spoke of a breakdown in his relationship with the committee. He did a good job but was too gregarious for some tastes and the image in my mind is of his half-full pint on the bar, a cigarette burning itself out and bits of correspondence scattered while he went off to attend to something. The pavilion, built after the 1981 NatWest triumph, was a financial success under Pearman but his style was his own and it sometimes resembled a Working Men's Club. So what? He brought people in, they spent money, the atmosphere was cheerful and the social side did not interfere with the cricket activities. Pearman was upset by the severance because he felt he was making a success of the job, as indeed he was in many ways: the image ruffled the committee. The recruitment continued and Peter Bowler scored a century on his Derbyshire debut in 1988 against Cambridge University at Fenner's, his unbeaten 155 attracting more than usual notice as he had made 100 not out on his debut for Leicestershire two years earlier. He was an excellent acquisition, with 1,725 runs in the season, while Steve Goldsmith, another new arrival after being released by Kent, also passed 1,000 runs. Tim O'Gorman, who was studying law, again made a few appearances at the end of the Durham University term as the batting developed greater depth and there was a sniff of success as Derbyshire reached the Final of the Benson and Hedges Cup. They were unbeaten at the top of their group and thrashed Middlesex by nine wickets in the quarter-final at Derby, set up by great bowling from Michael Holding and Devon Malcolm. The semi-final, spread over three days at Swansea, was much tighter, tense enough for Guy Willatt, then cricket chairman, to seek refuge behind the rugby stand at one stage to avoid transmitting his nerves. A key moment came on the first day when Matthew Maynard, having set off brightly, lost his helmet when playing Holding and saw it bounce into the stumps like a cannonball. Sponsored lunches, laid on for the Press in knock-out competitions, were always a mixed blessing and, as the standard deteriorated, I opted for the pub across the road on day three. It looked an even better decision when the Bensons representative, having doled out his offerings, came and sat at the next table. Derbyshire flopped at Lord's in a one-sided Final. Steve Jefferies, a South African who played for them once in a match against the Pakistan tourists, swung the ball prodigiously in the morning and figures of 10-3-13-5 left Hampshire needing only 118 to win. Derbyshire batted feebly, failing to respond to the occasion, and the season tailed away from there, although we had already seen one of the great exhibitions of one-day bowling. Holding took eight for 21 to destroy Sussex at Hove in the NatWest Trophy and nine of the runs were from no-balls debited against him. When asked how it rated in his best performances, Holding said: "Not even in the top ten," but he was fearsome. The only tabloid journalist there on time to see Holding's glory was the conscientious and respected *Daily Mail* cricket correspondent Peter Smith. It seemed to sum up that world when, not long afterwards, he lost his job.

Holding's presence was an important factor in attracting Ian Bishop and, at the end of 1988, John Wright retired from county cricket. So did Roger Finney, whose all-round determination helped to establish Barnett's side before his ability to bowl deserted him. At the start, he swung the ball in at medium pace then, when he began to tie up, adopted a slower style. He lost control of that, too, and it became agony to watch him trying to bowl, as it had with Fred Swarbrook earlier. Holding had one more season and demonstrated his principles in an extraordinary match at Trent

Bridge. Nottinghamshire and Derbyshire were both dismissed on the first day on an unsuitable pitch, geared to seam at one end and spin at the other. Several Nottinghamshire batsmen mimed their displeasure on the second day and, having already reported the pitch, the umpires halted the game to telephone Lord's for further instructions. It was decided to continue the match on a different strip, causing a two-hour delay, and at that point Holding declined to take any further part as he considered the situation farcical. Perhaps through political expediency, Derbyshire later reprimanded Holding, who had the satisfaction of steering the side to victory over Nottinghamshire by one wicket in his final game at the County Ground. The batting gained fresh zest as Morris moved into maturity and Chris Adams began to make an impact as Derbyshire ended the season strongly. Adams, who completed his education at Repton School, was soon revealed as a fine striker of the ball and a breathtaking fielder close to the wicket. He, too, became enmeshed in Derbyshire politics and demanded to leave after 10 years, to become captain of Sussex. As the 1990 season opened, however, Derbyshire were building rather than demolishing and Barnett's first trophy was looming. Barnett was caught in controversy when he joined a 'rebel' tour to South Africa, then excluded from the international game. Demonstrators lined up outside the College Ground at Cheltenham soon after he and Gloucestershire's former captain David Graveney were revealed as members of the party, although the protest disbanded as lunch and the chance of a pint loomed. Anything to do with South Africa was politically delicate and, as a result of Barnett's involvement in what became a fraught tour, Derbyshire County Council withdrew their grant for youth cricket, thereby penalising the wrong people. Adrian Kuiper, a fierce hitter from Western Province, replaced Holding as the second overseas player and was a vital cog in the Refuge Assurance League success. He and Bishop could not play in the same team but the selection worked well on Sundays, especially after an inspiring start at Hove. Refuge took over the sponsorship from John Player in 1987, thus ending the supply of free cigarettes which, with the kind assistance of non-smoking colleagues, used to help me through the summer but the principle remained the same. Games of 40 overs could be diverting in their own right and, with a convenient afternoon slot, always had a following but if a team was to challenge for the top, early momentum was essential. By the end of June, it was always clear which counties had a chance.

Derbyshire beat Sussex with a fine flourish in the first game. They needed 78 from the last 10 overs but Kuiper and Adams hit so cleanly that they won with seven balls to spare. On my way home round the M25, I noticed a car had been pulled over by the police and, a few moments later, realised it was Barnett's. A vague thought that I may be able to help, impossible anyway, was quickly replaced by the more logical decision to remove myself from those officers as quickly as possible. It was the first of three victories before they fell to Yorkshire at Headingley, rapidly recovering in a magnificent match at Taunton. Many who cover cricket rate this among their favourite venues. It is not especially attractive and the old pavilion, now superseded by a more modern building at the other end, remains ramshackle but there is a good atmosphere, a pleasant view of the Quantocks and easy access from the town centre. The pitch is usually excellent, with pace and bounce, but Somerset's 258 for seven offered a formidable target. Barnett and Morris responded with centuries in a marvellous opening partnership of 232 but, when they were out, Derbyshire had to keep going. Adams went in as the non-striker when a single was required off the last ball, so set himself to sprint as soon as it left the bowler's hand. He was surprised to hear no answering beat of hooves, glanced up and saw Kuiper strolling towards him, taking off a glove and pointing to the Stragglers' Bar, over which he had flipped a massive six. Gladstone Small could not manage that when Warwickshire lost by one run at the County Ground, by which time Derbyshire were right in contention. The most important victory was over Lancashire, the eventual runners-up, at Old Trafford at the beginning of July. Set 250 to win, Lancashire batted all the way down and the margin was only five runs when Paul Allott was run out with a ball to spare. Derbyshire had a nightmare at the United Services Ground, Portsmouth, when Hampshire rushed them out for 61, but Bowler's expertly paced half-century saw them home in a rain-reduced game at Swansea. There was another exhilarating chase against Kent at Queen's Park. Kent scored 276 for four, during which assault Mortensen's eight overs cost only 23, but Barnett's wonderful 127 kept Derbyshire right in the game and after Morris hit 45 from 20 balls, they won with 10 balls to spare. The last two matches were at Derby, rain bringing both concern and relief against Middlesex. Conditions reduced it to 14 overs each, from which Derbyshire conjured 128 for five. With Desmond Haynes and Mark Ramprakash going well, that began to look vulnerable but clouds were building over Alvaston, a safe direction for rain, and when they emptied emphatically, Derbyshire managed to win on run rate, rather easier to grasp than the contemporary Duckworth-Lewis higher mathematics. As a result, Derbyshire would be Champions if they beat Essex, which they did with three balls to spare. Morris and Malcolm, playing for England against India at the Oval, travelled up on their rest day to share the tension and relish the celebrations. They deserved to be there because they played a full part in the triumph which provoked a rare sight, a pitch invasion at the County Ground. Barnett's batting and leadership were equally crucial. There were, too, unsung heroes, not least Bowler as a wicketkeeper.

When I wrote something rather sniffy about the lack of a specialist behind the stumps, he soon appeared, to point out that he did not particularly enjoy keeping but it was for the benefit of the team by enabling them to include an extra batsman. He was quite right and more than competent with the gauntlets. Simon Base was the leading bowler with 19 wickets at an average cost of 22.68. He performed with great discipline, not always a watchword for one so frequently near boiling point. At his best, he made the ball bounce steeply from just short of a length but became intensely irritated with himself when he strayed. "I need a screwdriver to release all the steam from my head," he said in a revealing moment and in one Championship match was seen biting a bail in sheer frustration, something later confirmed by an incredulous umpire. Warner usually bowled the late overs with courage and accuracy while if Mortensen took only nine wickets, he cost barely three an over. Everything came together splendidly and Brian Holling, who took over from Guy Willatt as cricket chairman at the beginning of the season, passed the credit for helping to construct the team to his predecessor.

Barnett's belief that Derbyshire could be a significant force in the 1990s gained further substance when they engaged the Indian batsman Mohammad Azharuddin in 1991 and finished third in the Championship, their best position since Willatt's team in 1954. Devon Malcolm played only a limited part in that because he returned from Australia like a wet rag. Ludicrously, for a player taken as a strike bowler for the Tests, Malcolm sent down 100 first-class overs more than anybody else on the tour. When the England coach, Micky Stewart, held a supposedly private but actually well publicised coaching session with Malcolm, Chris Middleton, the Derbyshire chairman, was openly critical and fined by the Test and County Cricket Board. It was hard to justify such a penalty on somebody whose work for cricket was on a purely voluntary basis, even if the TCCB were unduly and understandably sensitive about criticism of a faltering England regime under Stewart and Ted Dexter. John Morris fell foul of them in Australia when he and David Gower were each fined £1,000 for an escapade with two elderly Tiger Moths, which flew low over the Carrara ground to salute Robin Smith's century. As John Thicknesse reflected in *Wisden*: "It was a harsh penalty for an essentially light-hearted prank, reflecting all too accurately the joyless nature of the tour." At least it served Morris well when he came to design a benefit tie in his days with Durham. The new sound of the 90s was Karl Krikken endlessly rattling away behind the stumps. In no way did Krikken conform to the accepted style of keeping wicket, unlike Bob Taylor, who could have stepped out of a coaching manual, but he had wonderful hands and quick feet. For a decade, there were few, if any, better to be seen in the County game but he never had a chance at Test level. Dominic Cork also arrived with a bang. Derbyshire hoped to bring him along carefully but, as ever, Cork was champing at the bit and, after a few games, announced himself on his 20th birthday with eight for 53 against Essex at the County Ground. He was, and remains, a volatile cricketer but his ability to make things happen was spectacularly illustrated on his Test debut in 1995, when he took seven for 43 against West Indies at Lord's, following that with a hat-trick at Old Trafford later in the series. His intensity created the player but can also make him an uncomfortable companion in the confines of a dressing-room, perhaps a factor in limiting him to 37 Tests when his ability justified more. Azharuddin was a delight throughout the summer and Barnett, the author of several spectacular performances over his career, described his 212 in a comprehensive victory over Leicestershire at Grace Road as the best 'all round the wicket innings' he had ever seen. Azharuddin had a ruthless edge on the field as well as a complete array of strokes, backed by wrists of steel. He was wonderful to watch and, in common with so many Indian players, unfailingly courteous. It was with surprise and sadness that his friends in Derbyshire assimilated the allegations that he was involved with Indian bookmakers in the match-fixing scandal that brought down South Africa's captain Hansie Cronje. A consistent streak was developing and when Derbyshire were fifth in 1992, it was their third top six finish in four seasons. Bishop, who had played no first-class cricket for more than a year, assured Derbyshire that the back injury that caused him to return early from Australia in 1990-91 and miss the World Cup was clear. He kept his side of the bargain, with 64 Championship wickets at 17.46 and some of his spells were breathtaking. One at the United Services Ground, Portsmouth, sticks in the memory. With a claimant for the world's biggest roller, Hampshire often produced fearsomely fast pitches there, much to Malcolm Marshall's pleasure, but two players dominated the game. Bowler's unbeaten 241 was a marvellous innings, probably the finest he ever played, but when Hampshire batted again, 317 behind, there was a feeling they could make it difficult on a more placid strip than usual, especially with the stubborn Tony Middleton surviving into the last day. Bishop nearly took his foot off to win an lbw decision and destroyed Hampshire with seven for 34. It was one of three victories under Morris, in charge while Barnett suffered from knee trouble: that was quite enough to bring Barnett hurrying back. Bishop took six for 18 when Essex, already Champions, were rattled out for 96 at Derby. That was merely the prelude to an astonishing recovery when Essex scored 442 for eight in the fourth innings to win. Adams played the innings of an unremarkable Sunday season when he shredded Kent at Queen's Park. His unbeaten 141 was scored off only 102 balls and included 10 sixes, one calmly caught by Malcolm on the pavilion balcony. It was a wonderful exhibition of clean striking as well as power and he also passed 1,000 runs in first-class games. At the age of 22, Adams was a genuinely exciting prospect.

Barnett was already Derbyshire's longest serving captain, so there was some significance to his contention that the 1993 Benson and Hedges Cup Final victory over Lancashire was his greatest day. It was dramatic enough, the tension heightened by events at Derby a fortnight earlier. In a high-scoring Championship match, Derbyshire were set 379 to win in 89 overs and a brilliant 151 from Morris pushed them well along the way. Suddenly, from looking comfortable, batting became desperately difficult as Wasim Akram returned, made the ball swing wildly and took six for 11 in 49 deliveries. "It was the first time any of us had encountered reverse swing," said Morris years later as we watched a match at Quarndon, "and we couldn't understand why everything changed so suddenly." When Mortensen was last out, he chased to the boundary to retrieve a ball that looked as if a dog had been worrying it for hours and Derbyshire sent it to the TCCB for inspection. Astonishingly, it was concluded at Lord's that there was nothing wrong with its condition and Lancashire, it was said, resented the implied accusation of ball-tampering. They even managed to keep straight faces while declaring their innocence but there was a crackle in the air at Lord's, especially when Wasim hit Adams on the shoulder with a full toss. Adams was livid and disturbed the serenity of lunch with a direct threat to Wasim. Although blows were avoided, the exchange appeared to have some effect as the Pakistani star was, as they say, well below his best for the remainder of the innings. In short, he bowled rubbish. The road to Lord's began at Bristol in April when, with the zonal round scrapped, Gloucestershire were knocked out in a tight contest because, with the scores level, Derbyshire lost fewer wickets. Like Kent, Gloucestershire found themselves out of a major competition before anybody realised the season was in progress. Bishop played in the next round, at home to Middlesex, but it was his only appearance of the season because of a stress fracture in his back. He recovered after a long rest but, although he was able to prolong his Test career, that was the last Derbyshire saw of him. Warner's tight bowling, 11 overs for 29, was instrumental in sending Derbyshire through to a quarter-final at Taunton, where it rained for most of two days. Barnett and Bowler started solidly but the innings was declared void as rain persisted and the tie was resolved by a bowl-out. Having been knocked out of the NatWest Trophy by Hertfordshire under this method in 1991, a lesson was assimilated: don't let the front line bowlers anywhere near. It worked and Adams twice hit the unguarded stumps in a 6-3 victory, claiming both his efforts swung away, pitched on the off stump and nipped back to hit leg. Poor Mushtaq Ahmed, who sent down endless practice balls with a high ratio of strikes before the competition, never turned his arm because he was fifth to go and Derbyshire's lead was unassailable. The top four sent them surging past Northamptonshire in the semi-final at Derby, while Lancashire routed Leicestershire at Grace Road. Lancashire were clear favourites at Lord's and seemed to be in charge as Derbyshire struggled to 66 for four in 16 overs. Then Cork displayed his ability to turn games, this time with a national audience, as he surged to an unbeaten 92, eyes glittering with the excitement of the occasion. O'Gorman, to the manifest pleasure of a father obsessed by cricket, and Krikken supported Cork brilliantly. Lancashire's fielding became ragged and, when they replied, Michael Atherton batted in such a self-absorbed way that it almost paid Derbyshire to keep him in the middle. Almost but not quite, because he could pace an innings and, after an hour off for rain, there was celebration when Frank Griffith held a return catch to dismiss him. Neil Fairbrother was the one genuine threat and it was nearly dark when he came to the last over which Griffith, as it had gradually dawned on him, was to bowl. It was Griffith's moment of glory and he saw his side through for a result that was not well received by Lancashire. From what I saw behind the balcony after the presentations, only Mike Watkinson went into the Derbyshire dressing-room to congratulate the winners.

It was a great victory but don't forget this is Derbyshire, so there was turmoil in the background. Financial worries had gathered and, in May, chief executive Bob Lark was made redundant, with two of his senior staff also leaving. The honorary treasurer, Jim Crowther, resigned and, in September, chairman Chris Middleton followed him. At least Middleton left with a trophy on the shelf and, to his credit, continued as a regular supporter. The new chairman was Mike Horton who, in a hectic tour of sporting organisations, also became a director of Derby County and took over the Derby basketball club. To him goes the credit for redeeming the finances, although a legacy of £235,000 from Frank Stretton didn't half help, but there was never a feeling that Horton would have a long innings. There were stirrings in the dressing-room as Morris first stepped down as vice-captain, then sought his release to join Durham. Even more important to the running of the club was Philip Russell's decision to retire as coach and accept an appointment at Kingsmead, Durban. Russell, a steadying influence with his serene temperament, urged for some time that a successor to Barnett should be in place and Morris was one who fancied the job. So did Bowler, who left at the end of 1994 in a display of mutual animosity with Barnett as the winning Bensons team broke up. At the same time, Mortensen retired, in his case with thanks and good wishes on both sides. It would have been wiser for Barnett to relinquish the position in 1993, having achieved so much, because the next two years were miserable. I always tended to the view that strife in the dressing-room was relevant only when it affected events in the middle, if only because a dozen men forced into close proximity for around six months will inevitably have their differences. In 1994 and 1995, good individual performances seldom turned into team displays. Azharuddin came straight from Heathrow to score a wondrous 205 against Durham but 1994 ended unhappily for him because India wanted his services in August and Derbyshire withheld a fifth of his salary. The following year, Daryll Cullinan was made to feel isolated by a peculiar ethos of practical jokes unsuited to his serious approach. Colin Wells was engaged from Sussex to replace Morris and had a nightmare first season, ineffective with the bat and laboured in the field. At least he stuck at it and did rather better second time round. In 1995, Cork was an instant hero when he exploded into Test cricket. After the Lord's Test ended, Cork made his way to March for a NatWest Trophy match and spent most of the day fielding interview requests as the small Cambridgeshire town became a focus for national reporters. Barnett gave ample notice that 1995 would be his last season as captain and there can be no disputing that he emerged firmly in credit. The relentless focus that made him such a wonderful County cricketer carried with it an intolerance of lesser talents or those unwilling to conform to his specifications. His successor was an Australian Test player, Dean Jones, who brought Les Stillman with him as coach. They came from a difficult season with Victoria, where Jones lost the captaincy and Stillman's contract was not renewed, a likely indication that all may not be plain sailing at the County Ground. Nor, in the end, was it although 1996 was the most enjoyable Championship season I ever experienced with Derbyshire, either as an occasional spectator or a regular inhabitant of the Press box. They finished second, the best since they were Champions in 1936, but ran out of steam near the end, a draw at Taunton and a home defeat by Warwickshire.

Memorably, they won at Old Trafford after Jason Gallian scored an entirely unmemorable 312. It was the first triple century I had ever seen and, by definition, was an admirably disciplined innings, stretching into a sixth session, but even when driving home in the evenings, it was hard to recall any particular strokes. Derbyshire never recognised defeat as Adams, while still keen to leave, flourished, John Owen emerged from local cricket as a ready-made county player and Andrew Harris sent poles flying. Jones extracted significant runs from Krikken, to go with his superb wicketkeeping, and Barnett, who passed Denis Smith's county record aggregate of 20,516 runs, appeared to settle happily into the ranks. That was an illusion because Jones, hardly the most tactful, trod on some important egos but when the situation soared out of control in May and June, 1997, I was temporarily out of action. On my way to Highfield Road, Coventry, at the beginning of May, I failed to note some uneven pavement and fell heavily. It felt like a sprained ankle but I was able to do my work at the game and, in some discomfort, drive home, praying in vain that the lights on the road out of Coventry would not demand gear changes. Ann Brentnall, then the Derbyshire physio, had a look at the ankle and decided that my Achilles tendon was damaged. I was referred to Alex Cargill, who had put together, among others, Ted McMinn and Martin Taylor after serious injuries so, for the next eight weeks, one leg was encased in a massive plaster. The trouble boiled into open warfare after Derbyshire lost to Hampshire on a declaration at Chesterfield. Jones promptly resigned and headed home to Australia, leaving behind severe criticism of the attitude of senior players. Despite club instructions to the contrary, Barnett decided these needed to be answered in public and, while at Edgbaston for the Warwickshire match, went on Radio Derby. He was fined £500 but ECB regulations said he was within his rights to comment on the issue, as Derbyshire's administration should have known. There was now a gulf between Barnett and the committee as, in the course of four months, Derbyshire lost captain, coach, cricket chairman, chairman, secretary and commercial manager. Horton left the chair citing lack of committee support and, considering the chaos, DeFreitas did a good job in captaining the side for the rest of the season. Then he found out he was not even being considered for the job so became another highly dissatisfied cricketer, although he stayed long enough to take his 1,000th first-class wicket. A fine all-rounder and engaging companion, in 2000 he went back to Leicestershire, where his career had started, becoming their captain for 2003. Adams, who had been trying to escape for three years and even talked of taking his case to the European Court, left in 1997. However dissatisfied he may have been, he had a contract but Sussex offered him a tempting deal as captain and, a further blow, Malcolm joined Northamptonshire.

A structure built so carefully was now a bomb site and Cork, the captain for 1998, had a big job on his hands. So did Vic Brownett, the chairman, and new chief executive John Smedley, because there was another storm ahead. Derbyshire did better than expected in 1998, greatly helped by the emergence of Kevin Dean as a potent left-arm seamer, and surprised everybody by reaching the NatWest Trophy Final. They had no problem with Cumberland at Derby or, following Dean's three instant wickets, with Scotland at the Grange in Edinburgh. Surrey were favourites for the trophy but were convincingly beaten at the Oval as Derbyshire again bowled well. Barnett and Michael Slater, the Australian Test batsman, shared 162 for the first wicket to put Derbyshire well on their way, although Surrey bowled later overs so slowly that they clearly hoped darkness would envelop the game. The doggedness of the side was illustrated in a high scoring semi-final at Grace Road, where one of the features of Derbyshire's innings was 58 by Ben Spendlove, then only 19. He timed his strokes sweetly and if talent was not backed by application, there was surely something to work on. Despite directors of cricket and cricket managers, this seldom happened at the County Ground and any way of life not conforming to the orthodox resulted in players being written off. Even needing 299 for victory, Leicestershire created a winning position, needing 56 off 11 overs with seven wickets standing. Then Cork bowled Phil Simmons for 90, after which Barnett, with his underrated medium pace, and Dean bowled so well that they fell three runs short. It was an astonishing victory but the Final was the kind of flop one feared from the moment of entry to see the Lord's playing area under covers. When play began at 4.30, conditions and the poor light were just right for Ian Austin's nagging seam. After a decent start, Derbyshire collapsed rapidly and it was wrapped up by lunch on Sunday.

Before he left with England for Australia, Cork issued a statement saying he would not continue if Harold Rhodes, a former Derbyshire and England bowler, remained on the committee or Andy Hayhurst, director of coaching and development, had any say in decisions about senior players. Cork had, it seemed, been promised full authority over playing matters and while he was away, Barnett looked after his interests. Nobody could be better prepared for a campaign than Barnett and this one turned into a vote of no confidence in the committee, forcing an extraordinary general meeting. Changes were needed on the committee, as is usually the case with Derbyshire and several other counties. For a start it was, and remains, too big. The cause of strife was less sound. As captains develop in office, they have a greater influence on team affairs: through his achievements, Barnett became immensely powerful as captain. But it is folly and an abrogation of management responsibility to invest any captain with total authority. The greatest weakness was that the rebels had no shadow committee to step in so, when their motion was carried in the EGM at Pride Park, members were voting blind to find a replacement body. It was emotive stuff but even while the committee was being dumped, one member wanted to query a sub-section of the club rules. It hardly seemed the right time.

When the Championship split after 2000, Derbyshire did extremely well to qualify for the First Division. They did not stay long and had two dreadful years. Players continued to leave and, in 2002, there was a well equipped ex-Derbyshire side playing elsewhere, lacking only a specialist wicketkeeper. The Grandstand has gone, soon to be replaced by a cricket school and community facility. The County Ground looks in good shape, despite frequent jousts with Pitches Panels, but success on the field is far away. Barnett had his contract paid up and joined Gloucestershire, with considerable success, for 1999. They, too, settled with him a year early and Cork wanted him back at Derby in 2003. The cricket committee rejected the idea and a proposal to the general committee did not even find a seconder. Success would have pushed the issue into obscurity but the worst run of consecutive Championship defeats for more than 80 years meant it was not forgotten. The batting depended too heavily on Michael Di Venuto, the bowling lacked variety. There were not enough good players and, if Derbyshire are to survive, another reconstruction of the team is essential.

FOREIGN CLASS

BUYING out Robert Maxwell left Derby County short of money and players. They derived no benefit, apart from the considerable one of seeing off Maxwell, through the sale of Dean Saunders and Mark Wright to Liverpool, especially as four directors decided to realise their shares at the same rate. The team had suffered for close on two years because, although players of the stature of Peter Shilton, Saunders and Wright remained, essential replacements were not brought into other areas, leading Arthur Cox to liken the club to a car urgently in need of a service. The hope was always that somebody with a local affiliation would take over the club but when Lionel Pickering put in an offer, Maxwell announced that he was not a fit and proper person to undertake the running of the club. While it was an echo of a Department of Trade and Industry comment, some years earlier, on Maxwell's suitability as a company director, it was particularly rich in view of what was to emerge about the tycoon before long. Despite the size of Maxwell's empire, hopelessly overstretched by then, there was little doubt that Pickering could put his hands on more ready money. At least the Derby media made their criticisms of Maxwell and had their rows with him while he was still alive. Watching the *Daily Mirror* denigrating their former owner, once they were sure that he died after going over the side of his yacht, was nauseating. Maxwell wanted to call the shots at Derby right to the end, persuading separate bidders to amalgamate into an uneasy alliance, under Brian Fearn as chairman. The hope that all would settle harmoniously once Maxwell went was soon dashed but at least Cox was able to do some trading at a modest level. He bought two defenders, Andy Comyn from Aston Villa and Simon Coleman from Middlesbrough, who did a steady job in 1991-92. At the same time, he acquired two forwards on loan, the lanky Ian Ormondroyd, another from Villa, and a former Baseball Ground hero Bobby Davison, who had been sold to Leeds United. Davison was able to complete his century of goals for Derby but was upset when he was returned to Elland Road, Cox apparently having doubts about his fitness. As it turned out, a few extra goals from Davison may well have tilted the balance. It became an eventful season for Ormondroyd, signed permanently the following December then sold to Leicester City in March, along with Phil Gee, as part of the Paul Kitson deal.

Derby struggled along in the early part of the season but there was a complete change in November, 1991, when Pickering bought a controlling interest. After Maxwell, Fearn declared that the club should never again be in one man's hands but this was entirely different. Pickering was born in Ashbourne, educated at the Grammar School there and worked as a journalist in the *Derby Evening Telegraph* sports department before going to Australia. He returned home with a modest capital, an idea about free newspapers and a stout pair of shoes. In founding and developing the *Derby Trader*, he did the lot, from writing the editorial, designing the pages, selling the advertising to looking after the distribution. It became a massive success so that he was eventually able to sell for a figure estimated at more than £30m. He had always taken an interest in Derby County and was particularly fond of the 1946 FA Cup winning team. He saw buying the club as a way of returning something to a community that enabled him to prosper and was prepared to spend money to achieve success. After he had been there for two months, the buying began in earnest. Marco Gabbiadini, nurtured into an England B player by Sunderland but then in an unrewarding spell at Crystal Palace, was the first in, for £1m, and scored the winner on his debut at Fratton Park, Portsmouth. Paul Simpson, £500,000 from Oxford United, was a bargain, a creative left-winger with marvellous distribution who could also score goals. Steve Sutton, a Derby supporter when he was growing up in Hartington, had previously been on

Former miner Bill Copson played for England either side of the Second World War and had played in the 1936 Derbyshire team which won the County Championship. He was one of the first Derbyshire cricketers to capture my imagination

Derbyshire pictured in 1952. Back row (left to right): John Kelly, Arnold Hamer, George Dawkes, Les Jackson, Derek Morgan, Alan Revill, Edwin Smith, Arthur Hobson (masseur). Front row: Bert Rhodes, Donald Carr, Guy Willatt (captain), Charlie Elliott, Cliff Gladwin.

George Pope, along with Copson and Cliff
Gladwin, was one of three Derbyshire players to
win Test places in the scorching summer of 1947.

In 1969 Derbyshire bowled out Sussex for 49 in
the Gillette Cup semi-final at Chesterfield, then
the lowest score in the 60-over competition. The
damage was done by Fred Rumsey (left), Peter
Eyre (centre) and Alan Ward who, some years
later, made another little bit of history when
Brian Bolus dismissed him from the field after
Ward refused to bowl against Yorkshire.

All-rounder Ian Buxton, seen here pulling a ball from Surrey's Roger Harman at The Oval, skippered Derbyshire for 1971 and 1972. Buxton was one of a dying breed, the professional footballer-cricketer, for whom the publication of both sets of fixtures had special meaning.

South African all-rounder Eddie Barlow had the status and the personality to transform the Derbyshire team when he was appointed captain in 1976. Only strong characters flourished under Barlow's demanding approach to the business of playing cricket.

Bob Taylor pulls off yet another smart stumping to dismiss Essex's Norbert Phillips in the 1981 NatWest semi-final at Derby. Taylor also caught four that day and was later involved in Derbyshire's dramatic winning run. Three years later, after he announced his impending retirement, Taylor's appearances on away grounds took on an emotional tone as cricket followers turned out to pay their respects.

Derbyshire skipper Barry Wood with the NatWest Trophy after Derbyshire's memorable Lord's victory over Northamptonshire in 1981. Also pictured are Robin Leigh-Pemberton, chairman of NatWest, and Gordon Ross, cricket adviser to the bank.

Danish opening bowler Ole Mortensen pops the champagne on the County Ground balcony in September 1990 as Derbyshire celebrate victory over Essex and the Refuge Assurance League title which came with it.

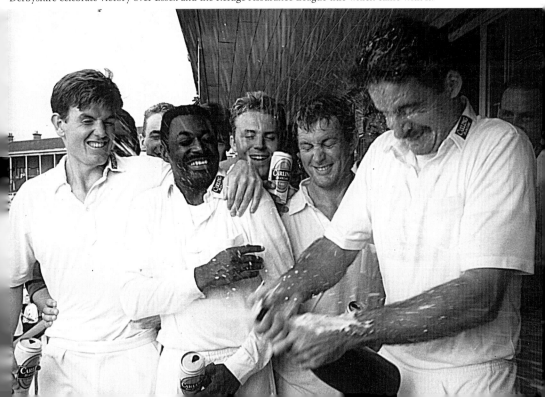

John Morris (left) and Chris Adams hold up the Benson and Hedges Cup after yet another dramatic Lord's Final when Lancashire were beaten in July 1993. Both Morris and Adams were among a host of senior players who left Derbyshire amidst dressing-room strife.

Kim Barnett was appointed captain of Derbyshire when he was 22. It was a brilliant decision and under Barnett the county enjoyed the most successful period in their history, with Barnett himself becoming one of the club's greatest-ever players. Sadly, his reign ended in controversy, not an unusual feature of Derbyshire, nor indeed of Derby County, down the years.

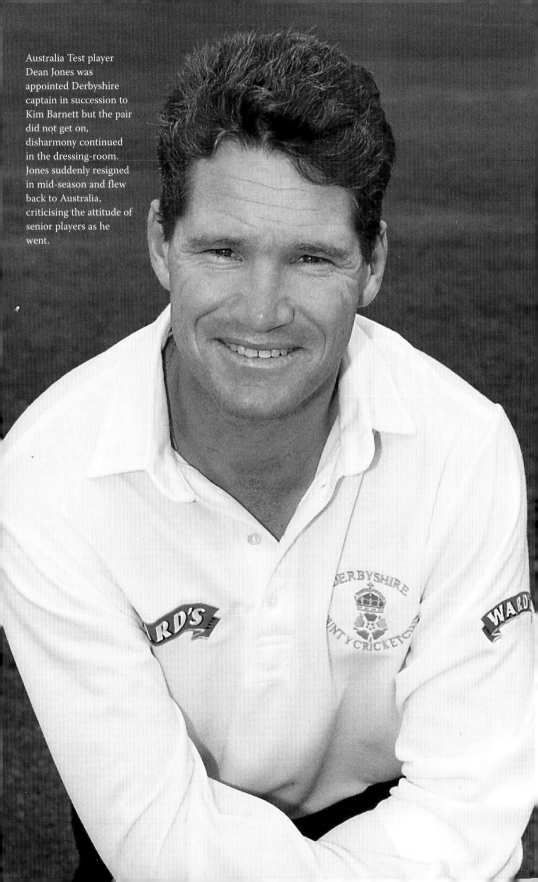

Australia Test player
Dean Jones was
appointed Derbyshire
captain in succession to
Kim Barnett but the pair
did not get on,
disharmony continued
in the dressing-room.
Jones suddenly resigned
in mid-season and flew
back to Australia,
criticising the attitude of
senior players as he
went.

Dominic Cork, was one of the most exciting young players in the country when he won a place in the Derbyshire side, and went on to a memorable England debut. In 2003, with the county suffering some humiliating defeats, Cork was not reappointed as captain.

loan at the Baseball Ground and cost £300,000 when Cox signed him from Nottingham Forest to strengthen the goalkeeping department after Shilton's departure to become player-manager of Plymouth Argyle. In March, Kitson and Tommy Johnson arrived for £1.35m each, with Leicester taking players in part-exchange for Kitson while Notts County accepted cash for Johnson. One player who interested Cox but did not appear for another decade was Rob Lee, then with Charlton Athletic. If there was excitement around the Baseball Ground, there was a bigger buzz at Ewood Park, Blackburn, where Kenny Dalglish was spending Jack Walker's money even more freely. Derby were 13 minutes away from promotion after the rapidly constructed team surged up the table but while they were beating Swindon Town at home in the last game, Middlesbrough recovered to beat Wolverhampton Wanderers at Molineux and clinch the second promotion place behind Ipswich Town. So Derby were in the Play-offs and made a brilliant start at Blackburn as Gabbiadini and Johnson put them 2-0 ahead after 14 minutes. Then they lost shape and discipline as Blackburn took over to win 4-2. It was an opportunity wasted and although Derby won the second leg, Kevin Moran's goal at the Baseball Ground was enough to give Blackburn a 5-4 aggregate. They beat Leicester, who were playing in the first of three consecutive Finals, at Wembley and were Premiership Champions three years later.

Despite blowing their chance, Derby derived encouragement and raised optimism about 1992-93, especially as the buying continued. Luton Town were persuaded, by a £1.25m fee, to part with the Wales international midfield player Mark Pembridge and defender Darren Wassall moved across from Forest for £600,000. Cox returned to Nottingham in September, this time to County for defender Craig Short at a club record £2.65m. Because the admirable Geraint Williams took a short cut to the Premiership by joining Ipswich, another midfield player was needed. Two signed, Martin Kuhl from Portsmouth for £650,000 and, a more speculative capture, Dutchman Richard Goulooze from Heerenveen. The blend which seemed close the previous season proved to be further away than ever and, despite 64 competitive matches, it was a thoroughly disappointing season.

The failure was at home, where they lost 10 League games, a return more associated with relegation than big spenders trying to reach the Premiership. When, in 1997, Derby left the Baseball Ground, everybody looked back to the great occasions there, the League Cup victory over Chelsea, Benfica and Real Madrid beaten in the European Cup. The arena could inspire players and intimidate opponents, especially when the mud was ankle deep, but this team found it hard to play there. The crowd did not react with open hostility, more glum resignation, but they expected more in view of the big fees laid out. So, reasonably enough, did Pickering, who discovered, not for the last time, that owning a football club can be a harrowing experience. Inconsistency in the League tended to overshadow achievements, progress to the FA Cup quarter-finals and to Wembley in the Anglo-Italian Cup. After squeezing past Stockport, Derby hammered Luton 5-1 at Kenilworth Road, where Pembridge scored a hat-trick against his former club. There was no presentation of a match ball, the feeling at Luton being that they had already given Pembridge enough over the years. Bolton were beaten in the next round but Sheffield Wednesday drew 3-3 at the Baseball Ground and won through Paul Warhurst's goal in the replay. The Anglo-Italian Cup was a silly tournament and attendances, especially in Italy, were minimal but I rather favoured it as a way of visiting places unlikely to figure on holiday itineraries. It brought together the English First Division and the Italian Serie B, presumably to improve relations between the countries after Heysel, but to reach the international stage, Derby first had to overcome Notts County and Barnsley. They beat Pisa at the Baseball Ground, then met Cosenza in Calabria. To judge by the holes kicked in the panelling of the corridor to the dressing-rooms, tempers had been tested in the oval San Vito stadium and it was no great surprise when Wassall was withdrawn at half-time with a stud-hole in his right knee. Derby won 3-0 but the most important thing for the players was to walk away from trouble, reminding us that, in previous incarnations, this competition was an unfailing generator of ill will. Derby's poor defending helped Cremonese to a 3-1 victory but an away win over Reggiana, sealed by a glorious goal from Gabbiadini, in the Mirabello Stadium saw them through to the English semi-final. That trip emphasised the difference between north and south Italy. Life looked tough in Cosenza but Reggio Emelia, not far from Milan, was a delight. Shops, clothes, the market and the food all confirmed stylish comfort. It was typical of Derby's troubles at home that they should squeeze past Brentford on away goals in the two-legged semi-final to earn another meeting with Cremonese. Most of the 37,024 at Wembley were from Derby but the result was the same as at the Baseball Ground, 3-1 to Cremonese, who were comfortably the best Italian opposition Derby encountered in the two seasons of meeting them. Nothing Derby tried in 1992-93 quite came off and while they had some talented players, a blend remained elusive. It would, because they had too many inconsistent performers. Gabbiadini could make life a misery for defenders on his good days, muscular, aggressive, always homing in on goal. On other occasions, the ball constantly bounced away from him but he had a long career through his underlying enthusiasm. It was impossible to dislike the cheerful Johnson, whose pace always made him dangerous, but he mixed spectacular goals with glaring misses, although that never stopped him going in for the next opportunity. Kitson and Pembridge gave the impression of being moody players but while Kitson's career failed to take off after Derby, despite a good spell with West Ham United, Pembridge continued at the top level. Short often looked as if he needed somebody to provoke him into top gear but if that happened, he was liable to become too excited. Kuhl was not a success at Derby and Wassall, who started so well, managed to collect any injuries going, especially to his Achilles tendon. Simpson was the most reliable because he concentrated on the things he did well but, curiously, was often the first to be left out.

The team needed time to grow together and, while there was no guarantee it would happen, that commodity was running out. Cox was under no illusions when he looked ahead to 1993-94, admitting that if there was no improvement on eighth position, it could well be his last season at Derby. He added Gary Charles, a full-back who played twice for England while he was with Nottingham Forest, and, in September, signed United States international John Harkes from Sheffield Wednesday. There was an advance but Cox did not see it through. In late August, after a 5-0 victory over Sunderland on the opening day hinted at greater prosperity, Cox fell victim to a back injury that prevented him from working. I went to see him at his home, where he was laid on the floor in a not wholly successful attempt to ease the discomfort. He was still struggling when he resigned in October, enabling Roy McFarland to take over. Cox was Derby's longest serving manager since George Jobey, having spent more than nine years in the post, and it was a sadly muted way for him to leave. For six of those nine years, he hardly made a false move as he rebuilt what had become a wreck of a club and his feat in taking Derby from the Third Division to fifth in the old First was the result of inspired management. Relegation was a bitter blow, the chaos of Maxwell's last two years seemed to drain him and he never appeared entirely comfortable with a free spending policy. Arthur Cox was, as he frequently said, one for evolution rather than revolution and would, I suspect, have been happier to move more cautiously. McFarland, who formed an effective partnership with Cox, was saddened by the events but had always wanted to manage the club for which he played with such distinction. He persuaded Alan Durban, another of the Champions, to join him and engaged Billy McEwan as coach. Although never strong contenders for automatic promotion, Derby won a Play-off place and engaged in a semi-final, memorable for all the wrong reasons, against Millwall. Gordon Cowans, with his first goal for the club, and Johnson scored in the first leg and it was already clear where Derby's advantage lay. They had quick players in attack, causing great concern to the ponderous trio of Keith Stevens, Pat Van Den Hauwe and Neil Emblen in Millwall's defence, so there was an obvious chance of more goals at the New Den. That was how it developed, as Gabbiadini and Johnson added two more in the first 22 minutes. A third, Van Den Hauwe's slow motion own goal past a stranded Kasey Keller before half-time, virtually ensured a place at Wembley but, by then, Derby's priority was to escape in one piece from the South East London. There were two pitch invasions, both extremely ugly as players were forced to hurdle flying boots and dodge punches. Brian Hill, the referee from Market Harborough, took the teams off both times, prolonging the evening by more than half-an-hour. Hill handled the situation brilliantly and cancelled a penalty he was in the process of awarding when the second invasion occurred. He ruled that, as spectators were on the pitch when Paul Williams fouled Clive Allen, it was invalid and restarted play with a dropped ball. Five minutes before the end, McFarland withdrew the two coloured players, Charles and Williams, later confirming it was for their own protection. As the end neared, both teams were leaning heavily towards the tunnel, ready to move sharply to avoid more hooligans. Any sympathy for Millwall, in their attempts to curb the uncontrollable, disappeared when Reg Burr, their elderly chairman, tried to blame Williams. "Mr Williams is physically aggressive and an unpleasant player," he said. "He provokes them." Williams, from Burton, was first seen as a slim left-back in the Youth team before filling out into a formidable competitor, either in midfield or defence. Neither he nor Cowans, signed from Aston Villa to add experienced quality, could tip the balance against Leicester at Wembley, although Derby were justifiably unhappy about the performance of referee Roger Milford, with his carefully coiffured hair and keen desire to be everybody's friend. Johnson put Derby ahead but, immediately before Steve Walsh equalised, Gary Coatsworth flattened goalkeeper Martin Taylor. When Johnson went through again, Simon Grayson brought him down with the definitive 'professional foul' but was merely cautioned. Late on, Harkes missed a sitter and Grayson was involved in creating the winner for Walsh. Leicester needed three Finals to make it to the Premiership but there was not much patience evident at Derby when Pickering said: "Roy McFarland will probably be manager next season or he might want to resign. I will ask him what he plans to do next year that he didn't do this time." It was hardly a ringing endorsement and, throughout 1994-95, McFarland was constantly harassed by rumours that various people, most often Howard Kendall, were lined up for his job. He also had to sell, Kitson in a messy transfer to Newcastle, Johnson and Charles in a joint deal to Villa. The big players increased in value and, during his time as manager, McFarland raised around £6.4m. He was able to spend more modestly, although one deal produced the admirable Dean Yates from Notts County, a classy defender whose career was interrupted at Meadow Lane by a severe knee injury. As McFarland's percentage of League wins lags behind only Brian Clough and Dave Mackay among post-war Rams managers, he was obviously doing a capable job but nobody, least of all McFarland himself, expected the contract to be renewed in 1995.

By this time, Pickering was chairman. He was initially reluctant to hold the office, despite his dominant shareholding, but felt the time was right to take over from Brian Fearn. For his part, Fearn wanted recompense for directors who supported him and expressed unhappiness about the power Pickering was embracing to make boardroom appointments as he thought fit. Something that should have been straightforward went to an extraordinary general meeting at the Pennine Hotel in October, 1994, and although the formal business took only 14 minutes to reach an inevitable conclusion, the atmosphere was horrible. One result was the return of Peter Gadsby and Stuart Webb to the board. They had been directors after Maxwell's departure, then stepped down to be associate directors and were finally told they had no role. After 25 years with Derby, Michael Dunford left in October to become secretary of Everton but the saddest event of the month was Martin Taylor's awful injury at Southend. Having overcome a sticky start to his senior career, Taylor was firmly established and the reigning Player of the Year. He was on the end of a rash challenge from Dave Regis and it was immediately obvious that it was serious. Taylor was carried off with a double fracture of his left shin and faced a long battle for fitness, including further surgery. He worked immensely hard but it was 29 months before he played for Derby again. After his release, he was able to rebuild a considerable career with Wycombe Wanderers, finally retiring at the age of 36. The important job in the summer of 1995 was to find a manager and, after a number of candidates passed through, Derby made a good choice. Barry Fry popped up, only to earn an improved contract with Birmingham City, Brian Horton was interviewed twice, Mike Walker once, there was a strong suggestion of Steve Bruce as player-manager, with Mark Hughes as his assistant, and Pickering had a yen for Osvaldo Ardiles. After all the speculation, Jim Smith suddenly emerged as the chosen man and, having expressing surprise at the muted atmosphere of his initial Press conference, set about reshaping the team. His first move proved inspired, the engagement of Steve McClaren from Oxford United as coach. Injuries curtailed McClaren's playing career after he left Derby and he began to find his way as a coach with Oxford's junior sides. Smith, who retained a house in Woodstock from his time at the Manor Ground, was aware of McClaren's potential and they formed an ideal partnership, Smith calling on 23 years as a League manager while being flexible enough to allow McClaren scope to try out his ideas. Several worked well but, if a new initiative led nowhere, McClaren was prepared to abandon it and explore elsewhere. There was no pressure on Smith for instant success but he had strong bargaining cards because Pembridge, Short and Williams wanted to go, thus offering a chance of substantial transfer income as well as shrewd part-exchange deals. The first signing was goalkeeper Russell Hoult, who performed impressively under McFarland while on loan from Leicester City. Pembridge moved to Sheffield Wednesday for £900,000 and Smith did especially well out of Short's money-back £2.65m transfer to Everton because he was able to acquire Gary Rowett, rated at £300,000 in the deal. In the same way Sean Flynn, an aggressive midfield player, was the bonus in Williams' £1m move to Coventry. Ron Willems, a clever Dutch forward, joined Derby from Grasshopper of Zurich, Smith went back to Portsmouth, who sacked him earlier in the year, for Darryl Powell and the chance to take striker Lee Mills helped persuade Port Vale to sell Robbie van der Laan. David Preece, released by Luton, added further experience in midfield, although Derby found they had to pay a small fee and Preece soon fell out of favour. The activity stirred interest and the feeling was that Derby were capable of competing. They also strengthened the administrative with Keith Loring, from Brentford, as chief executive and Keith Pearson, who had long service with Wolverhampton Wanderers, as secretary. There may have been a whole new look but Derby started slowly, with only one win in the first six games. At the end of September, when Derby were losing to Barnsley at Oakwell, there were shouts of 'Smith out' from some of the fans. The manager was unmoved: "It's a bit early for that," he said. He found one unexpected bonus already on the staff when Dean Sturridge began to score goals and worry defences with his spectacular speed. Sturridge always looked dangerous in the Youth team but could have left Derby the previous season, when he went on loan to Torquay United as a way of smoothing Paul Trollope's path in the opposite direction. Sturridge, small and powerful, obviously had something and Smith was about to bring the best from him but it still had the air of a year of consolidation until a major deal at the end of October. Igor Stimac, centre-half in a powerful Croatia side, agreed to join Derby from Hajduk Split for £1.57m. Where Willems had apologised for uncertain English – "because I have been speaking Switzer-Deutsch for two years" – Stimac knew only a few words. Six or seven weeks later, he was fluent, again emphasising how lazy the English are about learning anybody else's language. Stimac's debut in a 5-1 defeat was a disaster, although not entirely unexpected as Tranmere Rovers always beat Derby at Prenton Park, usually helped by goals from John Aldridge. That was on November 4: Derby did not lose again in the League until March 9, a run of 20 games without defeat that gave them the basis for promotion. John Harkes no longer figured by then. Smith replaced him after 33 minutes at Portsmouth and admitted, when questioned, that he should have made the decision a quarter-of-an-hour earlier. The American international never played again for Derby and, once Stimac arrived, a settled team developed. Stimac's immense self-belief spread to others and there was a solid central frame, with Yates his partner at the back, Powell and van der Laan cease-lessly energetic in central midfield. Powell had his critics until the day he left and, with his long legs, could be clumsy on the ball but he had an immense heart. So did van der Laan, who was also a natural leader and a tremendous personality. He was with Port Vale for long enough to sound more Potteries than Dutch and earned immortality with the winner against Crystal Palace on the day when Derby made sure of their Premiership place. Smith appeared to think van der Laan's job was done once they left Division One and allowed him out on loan to Wolves the following season. Trollope went on even more of a tour but they returned and were absolutely vital in preserving the status through a difficult first season. Stimac, though, was the catalyst. Smith asked him if he could play on the right as well as the left in defence and later reported: "Igor looked at me as if I'd gone out." He was wonderful, great ability and immense charm, although he irritated opponents with what they saw as arrogance. Smith was able to add to his squad at the end of January by signing Chris

Powell from Southend United for £800,000. The left-back began diffi-dently but became one of the crowd's favourites, so that nobody could ever understand why he was sold to Charlton Athletic in 1998. Powell did not want to leave but, while he was at the Valley, earned England caps includ-ing, to his pleasure, a substitute appearance against Mexico at Pride Park. Nor could Smith ever find an adequate replacement.

After the defeat at Tranmere, Derby had a wonderful run of 10 victo-ries in 11 matches, broken only by a draw with Crystal Palace at Selhurst Park. At times, they dismissed the opposition but the longer an unbeaten run continues, the more edgy performances tend to become. They were still picking up points and also showed a sense of theatre by announcing, before a home draw with Luton Town, that they would be building a new stadium. There was talk of this in 1992 with a site identified, at Chaddesden Sidings. A company called StadiVarios offered an attractive deal but, to my knowledge, never erected a stadium anywhere. So Derby fell back on redeveloping the Baseball Ground, with plans in place, until the City Council's regeneration project at Pride Park, much the same loca-tion as originally proposed, felt the need of a centrepiece. The value of Gadsby, who ran a construction company, was then evident, the land was acquired at a good price and the most important decision of Pickering's chairmanship was taken. Going up would increase the potential benefit of the move and there were a few awkward moments. Simpson remembers a point-saving penalty, at home to Watford, as one of the most testing moments of a long career. He tucked away another for an important victory at Oldham and followed it with a hat-trick against Tranmere: like Alan Hinton, he had considerable mental strength. All would be decided in the final home match, against Crystal Palace with a full house of 17,000. If Derby won, there were up behind Sunderland and were off to a great start when Simpson put Sturridge away to score in the second minute. Kenny Brown soon equalised but, after 63 minutes, van der Laan headed in Simpson's corner and, this time, Derby held their lead. It was fitting that van der Laan should decide it, because of the way he lifted the team on the field, just as it was right that Sturridge should score and complete 20 League goals for the season in the final game at West Bromwich. Nobody had done that since Bobby Davison 11 years earlier. Yates was the Player of the Year and Smith rightly basked in the credit. "He's put a smile back on the faces of Derby people," said Brian Clough, "and that includes me because I've made my home here." It was the first of four very good years for Smith, who was aware of the need to raise standards for the Premiership and looked abroad. Having Stimac in the club helped him to sign Aljosa Asanovic, also from Hajduk Split, and he went to Denmark for Silkeborg defender Jacob Laursen. Croatia and Denmark were in England for the 1996 European Championship finals, giving Derby supporters a chance to see their new men. Laursen was on the fringe of Denmark's side but Asanovic was absolutely central to the excellent Croatia team and Smith was able to sit smugly at a friendly in Dublin before the tournament while Asanovic alerted managers and scouts with his class. Croatia were brilliant when they beat Denmark at Hillsborough, Stimac swaggering at the back, Asanovic dropping passes from any range and a sublime forward, Davor Suker, who chipped Peter Schmeichel for one of the great goals. Stimac was less distinguished in the quarter-final, sent off in an ill-tempered and abysmally refereed game against Germany, but there was much to savour for the final season at the Baseball Ground, especially as Smith added the versatile Christian Dailly from Dundee United. Although his transfer dealings did not slip into the red until Ashley Ward was purchased from Norwich City to beat the 1996 deadline, boardroom backing in the summer helped to produce a team good enough to stay up. There were some great moments, such as Laursen's shell to beat Schmeichel in the 1-1 home draw with Manchester United or Sturridge's wonderful goal in a 2-2 at Highbury. Sturridge came across Arsenal captain Tony Adams and let fly for that most visually satisfying of goals, the one that smacks the underside of the bar and rockets up to bulge the roof of the net. Further experience was added by the capture of Paul McGrath from Aston Villa. McGrath was 36 when he arrived, his knees were wrecked and he was wonderful. His idea of training was a gentle trundle round Raynesway before telling the manager that he did not head balls on a Friday and there was no point in pushing him into anything more strenuous. McGrath, so gentle and quietly spoken, knew what he had to do to be ready for games and how to get through them. When Derby played Wimbledon at Selhurst Park in January, he hit an awful pass across the face of the area to put Efan Ekoku, one of the fastest, if not among the best, players in the League clear on goal. McGrath realised what he had done and, with a burst of pace that would have been astonishing in a man at the peak of fitness, ran back and past Ekoku to recover the ball. When the Villa fans were at Derby for an FA Cup tie, most of their cheers were for McGrath. After an abandonment, Derby beat Gillingham at the Priestfield Stadium in the Cup and van der Laan, back from exile, scored the second goal. Laursen was injured in the warm-up before Derby played Villa, so Dailly slipped in at the back with startling effect in a convincing 3-1 victory. There was greater drama against Coventry as Derby turned a 2-0 deficit into a 3-2 victory, Sturridge hitting in Trollope's centre for a late winner. Then they had a bad week against Middlesbrough. Russell Hoult had a nightmare at the Riverside Stadium as Fabrizio Ravanelli collected a hat-trick in a 6-1 embarrassment and scored again, past Martin Taylor, in a 2-0 Cup victory at the Baseball Ground.

Hoult was not then the consistent goalkeeper he became, especially with West Bromwich Albion. "When Russ has a bad one, he makes sure everybody knows," Smith grumbled. The manager had something up his sleeve and brought Mart Poom from Flora Tallinn just before the deadline. He knew the Estonian at Portsmouth, where injuries prevented the renewal of a work permit. At the same time, two Costa Ricans, Maurico Solis and Paulo Wanchope, joined Derby after a trial. We were close to one of Smith's best days, the 3-2 victory over Manchester United at Old Trafford in April, 1996. United had lost one League match at home in 28 months, Derby had won once away all season. But Poom was splendid and Wanchope scored a wonderful goal, running from inside his own half past and through the entire United defence before beating Schmeichel. Derby were nearly there and made absolutely sure by winning at Coventry before the farewell to the Baseball Ground, against Arsenal. As I was in a heavy plaster from my accident at Coventry, Keith Loring arranged a seat for me behind the Derby dug-out, where regulars were more than kind. The visitors' centre at Pride Park was in constant use throughout the season, although it looked the bleakest place on earth when Pickering laid the foundation stone. It was fascinating to watch its growth but if nostalgia ruled on the last day at the Baseball Ground, Derby did not, losing 3-1 despite Adams being ordered off after 11 minutes. McGrath, ending his contract, was replaced in the second half, applauded all the way to the tunnel and embraced by Smith. Everybody was grateful for his contribution. Having finished a creditable 12th, Derby looked towards Italy in 1997 and the new ground, as well as enhanced stature, helped to attract Stefano Eranio at the end of his contract with Milan. But for injury, Eranio would have gone to the 1994 World Cup Finals and everything about him was smooth, his football, with an instant mastery of the ball, his charming manner, his clothes. Even when he appeared in jeans for his first interviews, he was immaculate and, like Asanovic, he raised standards around him. Smith spoke to another Milan player, Roberto Baggio, but the figures on a potential contract frightened him off and, with a recommendation from Eranio, he went for Fiorentina striker Francesco Baiano and also signed Deon Burton from Portsmouth. There was every indication that the club was moving forward and there were 29,000 in the splendid Pride Park, which had been opened by the Queen and the Duke of Edinburgh, for a friendly against Sampdoria. The first League match was not so successful. Derby were 2-1 up against Wimbledon when the floodlights failed 11 minutes after half-time. They were eventually restored but only after the referee's cut-off point. It was especially galling for Ashley Ward, who scored the last Derby goal at the Baseball Ground and the first at Pride Park, only to find it wiped from the record. Before long, Ward was on his way to Barnsley and, despite his earnest work, was only a partial success at Derby. Baiano equalled a club record by scoring in six consecutive League matches, including two in the first victory at Hillsborough for 61 years, and when they were at their best, Derby were a match for anyone. Players were constantly away for internationals and Burton became a superstar in Jamaica, the island's Sports Personality of the Year, as his goals propelled them towards the finals in France. Asanovic, upset that he did not play, and have the ball constantly, moved to Napoli but was there in France, with Stimac, as Croatia finished third. Burton and Darryl Powell, who timed a late run into the team immaculately, were with Jamaica, Laursen with Denmark and Dailly in the Scotland team. Ninth in the Premiership, five players in the World Cup finals, an average attendance of 29,000 at Pride Park, where Derby were unbeaten in the League until February. They tailed away towards the end of the season and failure to earn a UEFA Cup place was disappointing but they were in the second tier of the Premiership, those who are comfortable and may win an occasional Cup. They went up a place the following season but it was in 1998 that Smith began to lose his certainty of touch in the transfer market. For a start, he signed Norwegian international Lars Bohinen from Blackburn for £1.7m at deadline time. Bohinen was a skilful midfield player but at Blackburn, and before that with Nottingham Forest, promised more than he achieved. It was time for Robbie van der Laan and Dean Yates, cruelly nipped by Dwight Yorke in a home defeat by Aston Villa, to move on but selling Chris Powell and Gary Rowett never made sense. It was easier to see why Christian Dailly moved to Blackburn because the fee zoomed up to £5.35m, too good to turn down. Horacio Carbonari, an Argentine defender of skill and presence, set a club record with his £2.7m signing from Rosario Central but worthy professionals though Stefan Schnoor and Spencer Prior are, they were certainly no better than the men they replaced. Tony Dorigo, back in England from Torino, added experience and, a bonus to journalists, was a fluent talker in the Chris or Darryl Powell class.

At the time, it was no more than an uneasy feeling because results were good and Derby claimed a rare victory over Liverpool at Anfield, only their sixth in more than 100 years. Enough were playing well, Mart Poom developing in goal, Jacob Laursen utterly reliable in defence, Lee Carsley and Darryl Powell endlessly combative in midfield, Paulo Wanchope unpredictably effective in attack with the thrusting Sturridge. Unfortunately, Brian Kidd left Manchester United and, after a long trawl for a successor, Sir Alex Ferguson settled on Steve McClaren. Smith told McClaren of the approach after the team returned from a 1-0 defeat at Old Trafford and knew what the response would be. McClaren is ambitious and nobody could turn that offer down so, although there was an immediate replacement in Ray Harford, a successful partnership was broken. I saw McClaren warming up United, slightly diffidently, before their next match, at the City Ground. Ole Gunnar Solskjaer scored four times as a substitute in an 8-1 victory and I wondered what on earth the new coach could add when they were back in on Monday. Some time later, he gave me an answer: "Luckily for me, it was an international week, so there was nobody there. I could not have offered anything new after that display." Vassilios Borbokis, a Greek defender from Sheffield United, was a curious signing in March and soon proved out of his depth in the Premiership. The Blades did better from a three-man deal as one ingredient was Rob Kozluk but the third man, Jonathan Hunt, faded as he had at Derby. Mikkel Beck was even more startling. Although the striker was a Danish international, few had seen him do anything other than struggle at Middlesbrough. It was almost a reaction to the failure to land Seth Johnson from Crewe Alexandra. Johnson was determined to do his bit in keeping Crewe in the First Division and, having accomplished that, joined Derby in the summer. At the same time Blackburn, who were unable to maintain their Premiership place, paid £3.5m for Carsley. It was a tempting fee but Carsley, developed through the Youth team, was maturing into an excellent player and Derby found it hard to replace him, especially as Borbokis and Beck were virtually given away. The FA Cup interested Derby in 1998-99 but, having slipped past Plymouth Argyle, Swansea City and, following a replay, Huddersfield Town, Arsenal knocked them out at Highbury through Kanu's late goal. Derby finished eighth and, although we did not realise it at the time, the good days were over.

Although Johnson, highly rated as an England Under-21 international, signed from Crewe for £2.5m, more good players went out and Harford, unwilling to move house to Derby, was replaced as coach by Malcolm Crosby. Stimac, not seen much in the season after the World Cup because of injuries, went to West Ham United, as did Wanchope. The Bosman ruling, that gave players freedom to move at the end of contracts, was at the heart of the Wanchope sale. He was reluctant to sign a new deal, so Derby faced the possibility of losing him for nothing in 2000: it was thought better to take £3m from West Ham but Smith was reluctant to sell a unique talent. Wanchope could baffle opponents and, almost as often, his own players, but moments of magic, plus goals, were the justification. He was a great signing, from Costa Rican side Herediano, and never flourished to the same extent when he left Pride Park. Esteban Fuertes, an Argentine with Colon de Santa Fe, was supposed to be the replacement and it looked as if Derby had signed him on their miserable pre-season trip to the United States. It was related to the sale of John Harkes to the North American Federation four years earlier but it was a long way to go for two games. One was against the US national team and staged in the accurately named Mile High Stadium, Denver, because they were looking for work at altitude before playing in Mexico. That was hardly relevant to a Premiership season and while Derby were in Denver, Fuertes' representatives arrived. Two clubs and a group of agents owned a piece of Fuertes, so there were complications from the start and Smith's temper became markedly shorter. He had already been irritated by training facilities in Chicago, to which Derby returned for their other game, and toyed with pulling out of the Fuertes deal. Later, he wished he had. Fuertes was not cleared to play until late August, was sent off against Bradford City a month later and scored twice in 10 appearances. There was no chance to see if he could make a lasting impact because in November, as Derby returned from a training break in Portugal, Fuertes was prohibited from re-entering Britain. His passport, acquired on the grounds that he had Italian antecedents, was discovered to be a forgery. It smacked of a tip-off to immigration officials at Heathrow and it was the last Derby saw of him. Fuertes went back to Colon on loan and, the following summer, was sold to Lens. That enabled Derby to recoup their outlay, but the affair threw a spanner into their season. They were permanently around the relegation area and it did not help when Eranio had his leg broken by Sami Hyypia's tackle in a 2-0 defeat at Liverpool. Smith was furious that the defender escaped punishment by Uriah Rennie, usually one of the better Premiership officials. Derby needed an injection of new talent, especially as Lee Morris, signed from Sheffield United, broke a bone in his foot in only his third appearance. Smith found two creative midfield players on loan, Avi Nimni from Maccabi Tel Aviv and Giorgi Kinkladze from Ajax. Kinkladze's appearance threw me, because we always checked transfer rumours with Smith and he never lied. There were two responses, either "Absolute bollocks, I don't know where this crap comes from," or a kind of strangled silence. The second reaction meant it was worth pressing on through the stages: "He is one we've asked about," was the start and, piece by piece, it gradually emerged the player would be there the following day. Smith dismissed the Kinkladze rumours but, two days later, the former Manchester City player was at Raynesway. At Ajax, he had been told to train with the Youth team and they were desperate to move him out so, when he signed permanently in April, £3m seemed excessive. There were two other £3m signings before Christmas, Craig Burley from Celtic and Branko Strupar, a Croatian striker who became a naturalised Belgian after helping Genk to the title. Burley added class and some goals to midfield: Strupar, who attracted hundreds of fans from Belgium to Pride Park, was a natural scorer and a delightful man. He could have been a major asset had his time at Derby not been blighted by injuries and operations. It was agony to watch him constantly fighting back. It was an expensive year for Derby who, in not much more than 12 months, spent close on £17m but if fees became a strain, the more constant drip was an escalating wage bill. Survival and, therefore, the television money was essential and Derby put together enough points to stay up, helped by Wimbledon's dramatic spiral under Norwegian manager Egil Olsen.

There was promise for the future. Johnson had a good, energetic first season and Malcolm Christie, signed only a few months after Nuneaton Borough took him from the Peterborough Sunday League, was a prospect. Christie looked about 15 when he first appeared at Raynesway but he had strong legs, tremendous pace and a habit of scoring spectacular goals. Like all young players, though, Johnson and Christie needed to be in a more stable team. Having apparently established themselves in the Premiership, they were back among the strugglers, striving only to stay up, and boardroom unity went out of the window when Peter Gadsby sued Stuart Webb for libel. Webb resigned before the case was heard and an out-of-court settlement reached. Before 2000-01, Derby managed to find enough cash to sign Bjorn-Otto Bragstad and Danny Higginbotham. Bragstad had a miserable time, although his pedigree appeared sound, an international and a frequent Norwegian Champion with Rosenborg. He had a terrible start and never recovered: Higginbotham, a Manchester United Reserve, began equally badly but buckled down with great resolution and was a Player of the Year before he left Pride Park. Jacob Laursen returned to Denmark in 2000 after 153 games for Derby. He was an exemplary professional, consistently efficient and the best-dressed man at the club. He expected to play every minute of every game, in contrast to Stimac, who began from the premise that was impossible. If Laursen was missing, everybody knew it was a major injury. Smith had to try everything to redeem the season because, without a victory until their 14th League game, Derby were early relegation certainties. He pulled a rabbit from the hat when, in November, he persuaded Taribo West to sign for the rest of the season. The Nigerian centre-half, a free agent after playing for both Milan clubs, was a colossal talent, able to dominate at the stroll with the confidence of an Igor Stimac. It was akin to the signing of Paul McGrath in the first Premiership season but there were more problems with West because when he went off to play for Nigeria, nobody was ever sure when he would return. Smith's patience was stretched when West failed to appear for a Tuesday night game at Charlton but the manager had to bite his lip. Stefan Schnoor went to Wolfsburg in exchange for Scottish international Brian O'Neil, who never quite recovered from being whacked across the knee by Roy Keane during his debut and Smith tried to solve his backroom problem by engaging Colin Todd as his assistant. First, he had to prise him away from Swindon Town, where he was manager, but the return of an undoubted great from Derby's Championship teams seemed to promise well. There was an improvement in the defending and Derby again managed to clamber out of trouble. They made absolutely sure with a remarkable win at Old Trafford, earned by Christie's wonderful goal. They were there at the right time as Manchester United were already Champions and, after the game, there was the usual tacky Premiership presentation. Derby did well to stay up and, in May, England beat Mexico at Pride Park, the first full international in Derby since 1911. The demise of Wembley took England around the country to enthusiastic venues and it was another mark of Derby's progress. Smith tried to keep it going on the field by chasing Fabrizio Ravanelli, available on a free transfer from Lazio. It was anything but cheap as, after various hitches were resolved, Ravanelli agreed a two year contract at £40,000-a-week, the kind of expenditure that could only be justified by a rise up the Premiership and they had to bring in money elsewhere by selling Rory Delap to Southampton for £4m. When Derby went to Estonia, part of the Poom deal, and Finland in pre-season, Smith admitted it could be his most difficult season so far. He did not realise how little of it he would see as Derby had three managers in 2001-02, an infallible recipe for the relegation that overtook them. Perhaps Steve Round, who succeeded Malcolm Crosby as coach, and Eric Steele knew something. They left in summer, Round to work with Steve McClaren, by then manager of Middlesbrough, and Steele to become Aston Villa's goalkeeping coach. Derby beat Blackburn on the opening day and Ravanelli scored with an immaculate free kick but it was not a sign of good things to come. Ravanelli created tremendous interest as an instantly recognisable player and played well for half-a-season but the point was that Derby could not afford him. After seven matches brought only five points, Smith left and Colin Todd succeeded him. The board hoped Smith would stay as Director of Football but Todd made it clear he did not want him at the training ground. "I'd have been like a spare prick at the wedding," said Smith and, clearly upset at the turn of events, decided to leave. To allow him to bring in Ravanelli, then sack him after seven League games was patent nonsense. There was a case to be made for Derby releasing Smith earlier but, having extended his contract, it smacked of panic to push him out at the beginning of October. He achieved great things for Derby and although the magic touch deserted him, they would have improved their chance of surviving had he stayed. Stefano Eranio, who had agreed to return for one season, was just recovering from injury but the treatment of Smith persuaded him it was time to go home to Italy. Smith had already set the wheels in motion for Seth Johnson to join Leeds United and the transfer went through in October, for a startling £7m. It was a great chance to add substance to the team but Todd brought three players from the French League, Francois Grenet, Luciano Zavagno and, on loan for the season, Pierre Ducrocq. It was impossible to have an opinion in advance as hardly anybody had heard of them but their contribution turned out to be minimal. Benito Carbone was on loan from Bradford City, who were delighted to be relieved of his wages, but remained a 'nearly' player. There were occasional flickers but a gruesome home defeat by Bristol Rovers in the FA Cup did Todd's standing no good and, nine days later, he was sacked after only three months as manager. It was an admission that the appointment was wrong in the first place. At the time, John Gregory was falling out with Doug Ellis and, when he left Aston Villa, Derby jumped at the chance to engage their former player. He immediately signed Warren Barton from Newcastle United and soon made it a double with Rob Lee after victory over Tottenham in his opening match. There was more life around the club and a glimpse of safety when they beat Bolton Wanderers at the Reebok Stadium in March. Bolton were awful and their manager, Sam Allardyce, was so upset that he could hardly speak. On the way home with my travelling companion Peter Green, we agreed that Bolton appeared to be doomed and Derby could scramble clear. Similar conversations were probably going on in hundreds of cars but Allardyce revived himself and his team to win three of the next four games: for their part, Derby lost the next seven and were down before my final trip, for a draw with Sunderland at the Stadium of Light. For all Gregory's extrovert nature, he was unable to change anything on the field and, in the background, finances were biting. Even before their fate was known, Derby had a rescue plan and players would have to be sold. Chris Riggott was likely to be among them, a Derby-born defender one hoped would be in the team for years. Smith gave him a chance and he quickly matured into an England Under-21 international attracting attention from several notable Premiership clubs. It was worrying, as was the lack of leadership. Earlier and justified plaudits for the achievements with Pickering as chairman faded into the past as he realised it was no fun being in charge of a failing club. He indicated a willingness to sell, specifying a buyer with Derby County at heart, but nothing changed. Webb, off the board, compared reports of the debts with the situation in the High Court in 1984. "We were sweating for £220,000," he said, "but that looks like a round of drinks set against these liabilities."

PIPE AND SLIPPERS

IT was business as usual on May 11, 2002, much the same as any Saturday in the football season for the previous 32 years. Peter Green was waiting near his home in Ockbrook and always stood opposite The Royal Oak, sparking calculations about how soon we could be inside it that evening. At the start, in 1970, I travelled with George Edwards, then Sports Editor and Derby County writer. For a couple of seasons, we were on the team coach before Brian Clough decided that the media section had expanded far enough. It was agreeable to wave grandly at friends from the coach but it was not good for clarity of vision about performances. Peter Taylor was particularly adept at slipping in his view, so it became a relief to travel separately, although I remember cadging a couple of coach trips from Arthur Cox, for night games at Gillingham and Wimbledon. When Edwards stepped upstairs, his deputy, Ian James, did not want the office, so I agreed to give it a trial, with the proviso that I was not going to be tied to a desk, in summer or winter. That particular balancing act lasted more than 20 years and, for most of that time, there was no assistance in covering Derby County's matches. Nor was it needed, as managers and players were accessible. It began to change when one Editor wanted a mass of useless statistics, even down to the number of throws, so David Parkinson was deputed to accompany me. There is only one relevant statistic at the end of a football match, the score, but it kept everybody happy. It was not, however, considered important enough for David to go on Anglo-Italian Cup trips, so I jotted down numbers when I remembered: anybody who

retained those compilations should regard them as approximate, as Jack
Mercer, for many years the Northamptonshire scorer, was wont to say. The
necessity for a companion came from increasing limitations on who could
tread where in football grounds and a greater demand for observations
from players, whether or not they had anything to say. The last two trav-
ellers, both engaged from the *Altrincham Messenger*, were Chris Ostick
and Peter Green. They were excellent because they accepted the limitations of the role and did not want to set their own agendas. There was a
principle, established during the Edwards days, of having a decent lunch
during a Saturday trip, just to make sure, should Derby be dire, that the
day was not entirely wasted. The custom appealed to Ostick and Green,
with healthy enough appetites to be life members of the clean plate society, although Green was happier than his predecessor to go along with my
more exotic tastes. There was nothing important about the game at the
Stadium of Light, except wrapping up the season. Derby were already
down and the only issue was to avoid equalling a club record with an
eighth consecutive defeat, achieved through Marvin Robinson's only goal
for the Rams.

No evening paper man had a better exit line than Neville Foulger, whose
last act for the *Coventry Telegraph* was to cover an FA Cup Final victory.
Although there was a kind note in the Sunderland programme, on the
'long and happy' lines, my last throw was like leaving through the tradesman's entrance and, a week later, it was all over. At the last home game, a
defeat by Leeds United, it was an honour that Brian Clough and Arthur
Cox should be there to share with John Gregory a private presentation to
mark 32 years. At the County Ground, when Northamptonshire went into
lunch on 39 for seven, Dominic Cork presented me with an honorary life
membership. The *Evening Telegraph* pushed the boat out and Steve
Nicholson, who had succeeded me as Sports Editor when, to my considerable relief, the decision was taken to have an inside man doing it, went
to immense trouble to contact former players and journalistic colleagues
for a farewell party at Pride Park. It was a great compliment to see so many
and some asked about plans for retirement. Plans? My whole life had been
a fortunate accident, with very little designed. Career paths were for other

people and if, like most who retire, I could have wished for those nice things to be said when reassurance was needed, there could be no complaints. For most people, work is a necessary drudge but I spent 42 years, in teaching and journalism, enjoying what I did for a living. It was possible to work as I did only because a succession of Assistant Sports Editors undertook the planning and design. Jeff Humphreys, an excellent wicketkeeper for Quarndon and tireless organiser of sports quizzes on behalf of the club, gave our pages a new look and others followed him, Steve Gill, Kevin Marriott, Simon Farrington, Mark Tattersall and Steve Nicholson. They gained good experience and many went on to better things. They probably felt they were better off with me out of the way but if many reasonably thought they should be in the top job, and paid for it, their support was marvellous. The juggling came to an end in 1994 when Mike Lowe, son of a friend on the *Daily Telegraph* sports staff, decided that the department should be run from the office, rather than by remote control. It was, on reflection, surprising that the change was not made years earlier but, once it occurred, it removed the feeling of guilt that occasionally nagged me.

One of the happiest sidelines was to be involved in the formation of the Derby County Former Players' Association, which stemmed from conversations at Reserve matches. Tim Ward was usually there and John Jarman, the community youth coach, was part of a similar organisation for former Wolves players. For years, Ward ran the Ex-Rams team, which had a full programme of matches for charity. We often remarked on how many former players lived in the area so, to test the water, I wrote something in the *Evening Telegraph* to say that the idea of an Association was being considered and giving a date when interested parties could turn up at the Baseball Ground to consider it. The number attending was not startling but there were enough to suggest it was viable and to elect a committee. Ward was chairman and Ian Hall the first secretary, now succeeded by Barry Butlin. The inaugural dinner, held at the Donington Thistle Hotel, was a tremendous success. Many people had not met for years and the buzz of conversation maintained an animated level throughout the evening. For days, Tim went round saying 'Wasn't it wonderful?' to everybody he met and the vital ingredient was his own enthusiastic personality. He was not well treated as manager but, like so many, retained a deep affection for Derby County. The Association was on its way and the dinner established itself as an annual event, now held at Pride Park. The other main fixture is a golf day, brilliantly organised by John Bowers and held at the Chevin Club, where they are the most generous and welcoming of hosts. John's occasional suggestions that the committee may like to consider other courses are briskly shouted down because it is impossible to imagine any other club would do more for the Association. Roger Davies undertook the organisation of the Ex-Rams team, something Tim loved doing because it meant he could have a game, or part of one, well into his 60s. Breedon Books, the Derby publishing company formed and run by Anton Rippon, sponsored the dinner more than once, to celebrate new books based on Derby County. Breedon headed an upsurge in statistical books about football with their *Complete Record* series, the first of which covered Derby. Rippon gave rise to the idea with a large format paperback history of the club, which he co-authored with Andrew Ward, Tim's son, and which he launched at the Baseball Ground. Raich Carter was among the former players present and it was intriguing to see that he hardly moved: others went to him. His hair was silver when he was still playing and he always had a remarkable presence. Rippon's book contained players' records and I had been collating them for myself for many years, initially to fill a gap in the office. It was obviously useful to know, for example, how many had achieved 100 appearances since the war and the task was comparatively easy at first because of a remarkable collection of cuttings books held there, each containing a season's match reports, teams and major stories. The first aim was to produce figures for the period since 1945-46 but it was impossible to stop there because Jack Nicholas, the Cup winning captain, Jack Howe, Sammy Crooks, Jack Stamps, Dally Duncan and others played on both sides of World War Two. Once back to 1919, the itch was to go all the way to the formation of the League in 1888 and this was more difficult, demanding trips to the Reference Library after work in the winter months. In the early days of the League, as many statisticians have found, coverage was not always reliable so, to fill gaps, there were trips to libraries in other towns, to the extraordinary British Museum Newspaper Library in Colindale and League headquarters at Lytham St Annes. Even now, odd doubts linger but there was enough to embark on the *Complete Record*. Mike Wilson, the club's official statistician, was an enormous help and should have been given a bigger billing when the book came out. His knowledge and doggedness were invaluable. At the time, Rippon did all the typing in a back room at his house in Overdale Road but was able to expand the business when the idea caught on. One year, we extracted the player biographies from the two editions of the *Complete Record* and expanded them into the 'Who's Who of Derby County', another swift seller. The second *Complete Record* was published in 1988, the *Who's Who* in 1992: so much has happened since that the time approaches for further editions, especially if ways are found to prevent websites from simply copying everything.

I have more time available, provided it can be properly organised. As is the case with many retired people, I seem fully occupied but would be hard put to quantify my activity. From being involved 12 months of the year, I was suddenly not even on the sidelines and it came as a shock. Watching the 2002 World Cup on television helped, even if it was not a distinguished tournament, but that was less important than continuing with a weekly column for the *Evening Telegraph* and covering some cricket for *The Times*. There is a danger of feeling washed up on the beach but the vast majority of former colleagues made me welcome when I looked in on them: only a couple were at pains to make me feel yesterday's man but, even if it niggled at the time, it was nothing to cause any concern. In essence, they were right and I remember a feeling of relief when John Woodcock, for so many years the best of all cricket writers on behalf of *The Times*, remarked to me how difficult was the period of adjustment. At least there was Scottie Cheshire, always ready to accompany me to matches which most others would consider irrelevant. He joined the Repton staff just as I was leaving but, because I did my basic training in the army with one of the headmaster's sons, I was back at the school more often than would normally have been the case. Scottie, a former Oxford Blue as a goalkeeper, was and is obsessed by football and used to organise autumn tours based, remarkably, around Blackpool. They were fun and I eagerly looked forward to making my debut after being released from the Sherwood Foresters in 1957. From him and an Oxford friend, Robin Stieber, I picked up the desire to visit all 92 League grounds which, with stadium developments, has become a target that has to be topped up each year. Cheshire and I are now occupied in trying to do them all in the current millennium. We're old enough to know better but we have some excellent outings and go in, disappointingly unchallenged, through the pensioners' gate. The majority of trips are in midweek because, despite spending so long at Repton and now living with an understanding wife in Staffordshire, he has a Chelsea season ticket, on the sound basis that he grew up in Sloane Square.

One of the strangest emotions was a sense of guilt if I did nothing constructive in the day, something I never experienced when in full employment, but many people reach the finishing line without being prepared for the next phase. After close on 60 years, interest in Derby County and Derbyshire would never wane, although both teams severely tested their supporters. Derbyshire set off so well in 2002 that great things were expected but tailed off sadly once Dominic Cork was recalled by England. That they are short of quality was even more evident in 2003, despite two outstanding victories in the Cheltenham and Gloucester Trophy, followed by a narrow defeat in the semi-final at Bristol. When Cork was not re-appointed as captain for 2004, he asked for his release and much depends on new cricket manager David Houghton. They have to build again, as do Derby County, who are hamstrung by a frightening debt. The 2002-03 season was about as miserable as it could have been, although at least it stopped short of another relegation. When I was still working, reconstruction was in the air. Peter Gadsby and John Kirkland resigned from the board, saying this step was taken to assist the process. There was also an intention to sell players during the summer but, instead, Derby were diverted by the involvement of former Coventry City chairman Bryan Richardson, who floated the possibility of raising a £30m bond. Without in fact being on the board, Richardson was called an executive director, a puzzling title, and faded from the picture before long. By the time Derby got round to selling in the January transfer window, the market had collapsed, so there was infinitely less money coming in for Mart Poom, Danny Higginbotham, Malcolm Christie and Chris Riggott. As there were a number of highly-paid performers failing to justify their presence, it was not especially surprising that John Gregory was struggling as manager. He arrived with such high hopes but perhaps it was a mistake to jump into the job so quickly after leaving Aston Villa. His suspension in March, 2003, amid allegations of 'gross misconduct' was nevertheless startling and when this led to his dismissal, Gregory instigated a court action for compensation. As nothing was said or written to explain his alleged offences, supporters were baffled but George Burley, as interim manager before his appointment in summer, conjured up enough points to head off the possibility of a second consecutive relegation. That was about the best thing that could be said about a dismal winter.

For two years, Lionel Pickering has sought a way out, originally with the caveat that he would sell only to somebody with Derby County at heart. By the time he opened the fine Academy and training centre at Moor Farm, the sole qualification was to come up with £5m. Difficulties arose because of his personal guarantees. The chairman, understandably, did not want to lose all his money and those who showed an interest in taking over did not see why they should pay anything to inherit a debt of around £30m. At least the big earners left when their contracts ended in June, 2003, so the outgoings were cut, but a massive struggle lay ahead. The outcome matters to thousands of people for whom Derby County is a big part of their lives. When I walked along Baseball Ground corridors in order to meet somebody, the thought often occurred that so many would do anything to change places.

I bumped into Jim Bullions, one of the 1946 Cup heroes, behind the goal when Derby played a League Cup tie at Mansfield. He was 78, still playing golf regularly, and said: "Still watching, are you? Well, you have to stick with it." He is right and there remains a buzz about a new football season, even when logic says it will be an uphill struggle.

INDEX